THE WHISTLEBLOWERS vs. THE BIG GUY

THE WHISTLEBLOWERS VS. THE BIG GUY

TWO SPECIAL AGENTS, THE BIDEN CRIME FAMILY, AND A CORRUPT BUREAUCRACY

GARY SHAPLEY
JOSEPH ZIEGLER

CENTER STREET

NEW YORK   NASHVILLE

Copyright © 2025 by Empower Oversight

Cover copyright © 2025 by Hachette Book Group, Inc.

Hachette Book Group supports the right to free expression and the value of copyright. The purpose of copyright is to encourage writers and artists to produce the creative works that enrich our culture.

The scanning, uploading, and distribution of this book without permission is a theft of the author's intellectual property. If you would like permission to use material from the book (other than for review purposes), please contact permissions@hbgusa.com. Thank you for your support of the author's rights.

Center Street

Hachette Book Group

1290 Avenue of the Americas, New York, NY 10104

centerstreet.com

@CenterStreet

First Edition: November 2025

Center Street is a division of Hachette Book Group, Inc. The Center Street name and logo are registered trademarks of Hachette Book Group, Inc.

The publisher is not responsible for websites (or their content) that are not owned by the publisher.

Center Street books may be purchased in bulk for business, educational, or promotional use. For information, please contact your local bookseller or the Hachette Book Group Special Markets Department at special.markets@hbgusa.com.

Library of Congress Cataloging-in-Publication Data has been applied for.

ISBN: 978-0-316-59659-6 (hardcover), 978-0-316-59661-9 (ebook)

Printed in the United States of America

LSC

Printing 1, 2025

This book is dedicated to the family, friends, and colleagues who supported Gary and Joe when they had to speak the truth.

Joe wants to honor his mother and father, who raised him to do the right thing, no matter the cost. His dad passed before this work was completed. Without doubt, Joe is living the principles he learned from his father.

Gary dedicates this work to his wife and children. Without their love and support, this challenging journey would have been impossible.

This book is brought to you by the whistleblower nonprofit Empower Oversight. All of the authors' proceeds from this book will be paid to the nonprofit to support current and future whistleblowers in bringing their truth to light. A special expression of thanks is owed to the attorneys who guided and assisted Gary and Joe to come forward and to defend the exigencies of their duties and promises.

The statements and opinions expressed in this book are solely those of the authors, written in their personal capacities and outside the scope of their official duties. They do not represent the views, policies, or positions of the U.S. Department of the Treasury, the Internal Revenue Service, or any other agency of the federal government.

CONTENTS

INTRODUCTION 1

PART ONE: CODE NAME: "SPORTSMAN"
1. BIG CASES, BIG PROBLEMS 9
2. WAITING (AND WAITING, AND WAITING...) 27
3. MISSING RETURNS 47
4. THE JUICE AND THE SQUEEZE 69
5. DAY OF INACTION............................87

PART TWO: OUT IN THE OPEN
6. THE FIGHT TO MAKE THE CASE 107
7. CAN WE ASK FOR A SPECIAL COUNSEL? 127
8. RED LINE..................................147

PART THREE: WHISTLEBLOWERS
9. BLOWING THE WHISTLE........................169
10. COMING OUT 197
11. AFTERMATH.................................213
12. BIG CHANGES 233

THE WHISTLEBLOWERS
vs. THE BIG GUY

INTRODUCTION

WHO IS WHISTLEBLOWER X? ... *Who is Whistleblower X?* ... *Who is—*

No matter where I looked in the small conference room, I couldn't help but notice the banner on the bottom of the television screen. The television was tuned to Fox News. Harris Faulkner, one of the network's twelve o'clock anchors, had just announced to her viewers that they would soon learn the identity of the IRS employee who'd blown the whistle on the government's various attempts to stonewall the investigation into Hunter Biden, the son of the president of the United States. I gripped the sweat-soaked copy of my testimony in my hands, running over the opening lines in my mind.

Today, I sit here before you not as a hero or a victim, but as a whistleblower compelled to disclose the truth.

Today, I sit here before you ...

I turned back to the television. By now, the media had obtained a copy of the opening statement I was holding. They knew I was a gay man from Atlanta, Georgia. They knew I had a husband in Atlanta and a family back home in Ohio. They knew I came from a conservative background and that I was now a Democrat. But they wanted to know more. All around me, members of Congress and their staffers moved through the Rayburn House Building with folders and iPhones in their hands. For them, this was just another day. People like Jim Jordan, James Comer, and Jason Smith (all of whom I had met just a few minutes ago) were used to intense scrutiny from the press. They were used to having their faces photographed a hundred times in a span of ten seconds and having those pictures broadcast to people all over the world.

I wasn't.

For the past thirteen years, I had been working as an investigator for the IRS. I specialized in healthcare fraud at first, tracking down people who fraudulently billed Medicaid and Medicare, often by running elaborate prescription drug diversion schemes or setting up shell clinics to siphon off taxpayer money. In 2018, I joined the International Tax and Financial Crimes Group out of the IRS's Washington, D.C., field office. The group is considered the SEAL Team 6 of the Internal Revenue Service, investigating tax cheats from around the globe. Naturally, I had assumed that the Hunter Biden case would be a slam dunk for us. Over the course of his career, the president's son had committed tax crimes that would have landed anyone else in prison a long time ago. He had concealed millions in income, failed to pay taxes for multiple years, deducted personal expenses like prostitutes and luxury hotel rooms as business write-offs, and used corporate entities to fund a lifestyle of addiction and excess—all while ignoring repeated warnings and opportunities to come into compliance.

But I was stonewalled at every turn. The Department of Justice, which was then under the command of President Joe Biden, clearly cared more about protecting the First Family than it did about seeking justice. Some of these agencies had become weaponized against enemies of the Biden administration, and career employees were so embedded that it was nearly impossible to get anything done. One of my only allies in seeking justice had been Gary Shapley, a supervisory special agent at the IRS who had a stellar resume, taking down criminals of all kinds. Over the course of the Hunter Biden investigation, we had been through enough highs and lows to last a lifetime.

The decision to blow the whistle on the federal government's stonewalling was not one we arrived at lightly. But we believed it was what we had to do. We owed it to millions of taxpayers all over the country. On the way to the Capitol from my hotel that morning, I had cried on my scooter—one of those cries that comes at you every ten years or so, shaking your body and sending you into the kind of convulsions that you'd be embarrassed to have anyone witness. Gary, I knew, had suffered from depression as well as a result of what we were doing. In just a few minutes, we would testify before Congress. We'd be open to attacks from millions of people, all of whom would know our names and our employers.

There had been severe abuse already. The FBI had contacted us both about threats from people who'd managed to figure out our identities even before we decided to make them public. We'd prepared for what lay ahead, but there was only so much you could do. My attorney, for instance, had someone comb through all my social media accounts, looking for posts that could be used against me during the hearing. I was relieved to find out that they didn't care very much about the "thirsty" Instagram posts that often showed me flexing in a Speedo on the beach. They were more concerned with posts about partisan politics, which were virtually nonexistent on my feed.

As mentioned, I was a Democrat at the time I came forward as a whistleblower. The fact that Hunter Biden's father was *also* a Democrat did not bother me. The right thing to do was still the right thing to do. The political affiliation of the person (or people) who might be brought to justice didn't matter to me or to Gary. We had simply followed the facts where they'd led. And, amazingly, that had led us here, to a conference room in the Rayburn Office Building, where we were about to be interrogated in front of the whole world.

At one o'clock, it was showtime. We walked into the hearing room as cameras flashed in our eyes. I tried not to squint. Amid the blinding bursts of light, I saw the people seated behind our table, mostly lawyers. I was grateful that they had come to show their support. But that morning, I was a little more concerned with the people who *hadn't* shown up. My husband, for instance, had sent a supportive text that morning, but I could tell he was pulling away from me because of the path Gary and I had decided to take. The leadership of the IRS Criminal Investigation Division was also absent. When Gary and I took our seats at the table, facing a dais of members of Congress eager to ask hundreds of probing questions, we did it knowing that whatever happened next, it was on us.

Five hours later, after in-depth questions from more than forty committee members, it was over. Representative Marjorie Taylor Greene had made headlines by parading around pictures of Hunter Biden doing drugs naked, pointing to them as she spoke about the double standards of the Biden administration when it came to human trafficking. During one of the many bathroom breaks—my handsome and capable attorney, Dean Zerbe, has the bladder of a six-year-old—I opened my phone to find more than four hundred text messages from friends and acquaintances. Many of them were people I hadn't heard from in years, decades even. My family, who'd been my biggest supporters through this whole ordeal, offered kind words. Even my brothers, who'd always made fun of how big my head was, told me my beard was looking good.

There were no camera flashes as I exited the room, and I looked down at my phone, hoping to see at least one message of support from someone in IRS leadership.

There was nothing.

To most people, such a momentous event would have felt like the end of something. But it wasn't. For me and Gary, the testimony was only the beginning. The threats would increase. So would the strains on our personal lives. Before that hearing, we were able to walk into the halls of Congress past dozens of reporters without a care in the world. No one knew what I looked like. No one knew my name. *After* the hearing, we were the two guys who'd blown the whistle on the president of the United States. That made us some enemies, and some unlikely friends. And it shone a light on the story we'd been hoping to expose all along—one about the son of a powerful man who committed serious crimes, then leaned on the federal bureaucracy his father controlled to conceal evidence of those crimes and prevent any serious investigations into them. Luckily, it's also a story of what can happen when people stand up against a vast government bureaucracy for what is right.

In the pages that follow, Gary and I will tell the story of the Hunter Biden investigation from the beginning. We'll discuss the earliest attempts by the Biden administration to stop our work, and we'll reveal many details that have been concealed prior to the publication of this book. In this story, we hope to make the case against the Biden family in plain English, walking readers through the exact details of the crimes and cover-up attempts. Although we will not shy away from writing about the severe personal consequences we suffered as a result of coming forward, we hope that our story will encourage potential whistleblowers to come forward in the future and do what they believe is right.

The fate of our nation may depend on it.

—Joe Ziegler, April 15, 2025

PART ONE
CODE NAME: "SPORTSMAN"

ONE

BIG CASES, BIG PROBLEMS

IT ALL STARTED with some half-naked guys in a hot tub.

Well, *photos* of some half-naked guys in a hot tub. It was early 2018 when Joe happened upon these photos for the first time on his Instagram feed, which occasionally threw him posts from strange people he didn't follow. From what he could tell, he was looking at a few male adult film actors lounging at a hotel in some far-flung tropical location. All around them was cash. *Lots* of it. The men clutched it in their fists along with bottles of expensive champagne, tossing it up into the air as they sipped. On the surface of the water, right at the level of the small bubbles and well-sculpted chests, dollar bills of all denominations floated by.

At the sight of such images, most healthy gay men in their mid-thirties would have allowed their minds to drift to some unsavory places.

But not Joe Ziegler.

As a veteran criminal investigator for the IRS, his first and only thought was: *Are these gentlemen paying taxes on all that?*

The answer, as Joe would later discover, was . . . sometimes. It turned out that the men in question made most of their money not from traditional adult films but a popular social media platform based outside the United States. For legal reasons, we can't disclose the name of it here. When it turned out there was substantial evidence that several people who were popular on this platform—which we will, for the remainder of this chapter, call "the social media company"—might not have been paying their taxes, Joe opened an investigation.

The next day, a few hundred bank reports showed up on his desk, and he started digging into them. For the most part, these reports made for dry reading. But Joe was used to dry reading. When you work for the IRS, you learn to trust your instincts when staring at spreadsheets and financial statements. Buried in all those columns of numbers were often the signs of a fraudster slipping up—a pattern that didn't add up, a transfer that didn't make sense, a shell company with no real business activity. Over the past decade, Joe had become highly skilled at finding those tells. Early in his career, he'd gone after doctors running pill mills and clinics fraudulently billing the government for procedures that never happened. He had traced dirty money through fake insurance setups and busted open multimillion-dollar tax shelters that spanned state lines. In the beginning, his investigation into the social media company looked like it would be another wide-ranging, mostly under-the-radar case. He'd follow the trail, document the violations, and package up the findings for the Department of Justice to review. Then it would be up to prosecutors to carry things forward.

But one day in November 2018, things turned on a dime.

The morning had begun slowly. Joe was running his middle finger down a line of black text on a bank report, checking to make sure that the amounts he was seeing were properly matched up with the names of the people he was investigating. Then, near the bottom of a page, he saw a name he recognized.

Robert Hunter Biden.

At first, Joe wasn't sure how he knew the name. That's how out of the loop he was politically. He remembered something about crack cocaine, hookers, and a Ukrainian national gas company. But most of those details were things he'd overheard on Fox News while sitting in waiting rooms or working out at the gym. To Joe, who was about as left-wing as a person could be on that first afternoon in 2018, all of that sounded like nonsense. He and most of his friends believed that these allegations were nothing more than conservative propaganda, carefully crafted to damage the reputation of former vice president Joe Biden. Admitting that you knew about this stuff—let alone *believed* any of it—at a dinner party would get you a round of weird looks and whispered asides as to whether you'd become a Trump supporter overnight.

But there was Hunter's name, right there in black and white beside the names of other potential tax cheats. As Joe kept reading, he discovered that Hunter's name appeared on these bank reports *a lot*, and not in flattering contexts. As the pages piled up on the left-hand side of Joe's desk, so did Hunter's potential crimes. For one thing, he seemed to be at the middle of a complex arrangement involving Russian prostitutes. He had paid several of these women allegedly for sex on more than one occasion, often using money from his corporate bank account. In tax cases, this is often the first red flag. People will live lavishly on their business accounts, purchasing cars and boats (and, occasionally, foreign hookers) with company money and then declare almost no personal income.

This, for any readers thinking of giving it a shot, is illegal. Don't try it, or we will catch you, even if it takes a few years. In Hunter Biden's case, it took roughly four years for an IRS investigator—Joe, in this case—to catch on to what he was doing. Which, when you think about it, is strange. Contained in the same bank reports Joe was now reading, there were references to news articles about Hunter Biden's many financial misdeeds. Many of the news articles cited Hunter's divorce filings, which contained allegations that he had tax issues for many years in a row. It took Joe about ten seconds of Googling to locate this quote from the attorney of Hunter Biden's ex-wife, Kathleen: "Throughout the parties' separation, Mr. Biden has created financial concerns for the family by spending extravagantly on his own interests, including drugs, alcohol, prostitutes, strip clubs, gifts for women with whom he had sexual relationships with, while leaving the family with no funds to pay legitimate bills . . . The parties' outstanding debts are overwhelming. The parties have maxed-out credit card debt, double mortgages on both real estate properties they own, and a tax debt of at least $300,000."

It seemed that many people knew Hunter Biden was not paying his taxes, and only a few of those people cared. Most troublingly, none of the people who cared worked at the IRS. Normally, allegations that people had serious unpaid tax liabilities came *from* the agency, not divorce attorneys. If Hunter Biden had been any other taxpayer, Joe was sure there would already have been an open case on him.

But there wasn't.

How did we miss that? Joe thought.

No matter how hard he looked, he couldn't find a single criminal case against Hunter Biden, who had by now failed to file returns for 2016 and 2017. Sure, this was only a misdemeanor, but it was still a crime. Anyone else would have paid for it. For a moment, Joe thought he had found a perfect slam-dunk case. He had more than enough evidence to open an investigation into Hunter Biden. Right away, he typed up a few notes and prepared citations to the bank reports he'd been reading.

In this way, at least, it was just a normal day at the office.

The last one he'd have for a very long time.

The previous month, Joe had joined the international tax group at the IRS. Although the name might sound generic, the group's work was not. This small band of criminal investigators and forensic accountants was tasked with identifying tax cheats from all over the world. They reviewed statements, sent subpoenas, and served search warrants. Occasionally, they got to kick down some doors. Unlike most people working at the IRS, they carried badges and guns. They had broad authority to open cases on anyone at any time.

Or so Joe believed.

From the moment he brought up Hunter Biden's name during a routine meeting in the middle of that first week, the reception was ice cold. There were so many sidelong glances and awkward silences that Joe began to wonder if he'd forgotten to apply deodorant that morning. Finally, after several attempts to talk around the issue, someone said he didn't think it was a good idea. For some reason, these tough investigators, some of whom referred to the international tax group as the SEAL Team 6 of the IRS, had become incredibly gun shy.

There was only one explanation, and it wasn't good. The IRS, which is an arm of the federal government, did not want to open an investigation into the son of a former vice president— especially a former vice president as well-connected and influential as Joe Biden. There were forces at work within the federal bureaucracy—and, potentially, within the IRS itself—that shielded the sons and daughters of powerful people from justice, even when those powerful people committed blatant violations of the law and did so, in Hunter Biden's case, with all the subtlety of a Fourth of July fireworks display.

Of course, that's not the explanation Joe got from his colleagues. What they told him was far subtler than that—and far more disturbing. During that first meeting, when Joe had just wrapped up his cursory summation of the facts of the Hunter Biden case, a fellow agent said, "I don't know, man. *Big cases, big problems.*"

Right away, Joe's Boy Scout instincts flared up. He wanted to tell his colleague that it shouldn't matter at all what a person's last name was; all that should matter was whether that person had potentially committed a crime. And since Hunter Biden clearly appeared to have committed a crime, an investigation needed to be opened. It was as simple as that. All we were talking about at this point, it bears mentioning, was *opening* an investigation, not throwing anyone in federal prison or even charging anyone with a crime. It was a process Joe had gone through dozens of times before, always without the slightest hint of trouble.

If this had been any other taxpayer, the process would have been simple. Joe would have collected the bank statements, written a report, and sent it off to the DOJ in a matter of hours. If he worked quickly, he could have done it all before lunchtime. But this was not any other taxpayer. It was the former vice president's son—who, oddly enough, appeared to be a tax*payer* only in the loosest sense of the term. If this evidence was correct, Hunter was a tax cheat, just like hundreds of other tax cheats Joe had prosecuted over the course of his career. Just because Hunter was doing it on a massive scale didn't make him any different. The fact that we were making an exception for him was ridiculous.

Unfortunately, Joe had never been great about keeping his mouth shut, so he *did* say all of that to his team, raising his voice at times and tripping over his words in places. And when he was done, most of his colleagues were speechless—and not in the *oh-my-goodness-you're-so-brave-for-taking-a-stand* kind of way; it was more like the *okay-we're-glad-you-got-that-out-of-your-system-now-let's-move-on* kind of way. There was some further light discussion of the Hunter Biden case, presumably to give the illusion that the team was actually considering it, then radio silence. It was as if Joe had never mentioned the guy's name at all. For the rest of that day, and the rest of that week, that one phrase played on a loop in his mind.

Big cases, big problems.

On one level, this was obviously true. The bigger the name, the greater the potential for bad press and screw-ups. Joe understood that. But he also understood that making exceptions for powerful people (and especially their kids) would only encourage more bad behavior in the future. He knew he needed to open a case. So he kept pushing. This involved speaking to a few of his superiors, most of whom expressed the same nervous lack of interest that his team had shown. Speaking to one of them, he said, "I really don't think the name of the person should determine whether we work a tax case or not, guys. It should be the merit of the evidence, the allegation, and the clear understanding of why we're opening that investigation. We should do the right thing for the right reasons."

That might sound like something you have the hero in a screenplay say at a pivotal moment, almost too good to be true, but it happens to be what Joe said. All his life, he'd been a rule follower. Sometimes, that worked to his detriment. But most of the time, it had worked in his favor. It was also much better than making a habit of *not* following the rules, as the Hunter Biden case (and some other cases he'd worked) had clearly shown. In general, doing the right thing was a good goal, even if you sometimes fell short of it.

But he also wasn't confrontational. When his superiors gave a directive, he tended to follow it. His worst nightmare was being labeled a problem by the IRS leadership, or causing trouble for the members of his team, who had always been helpful and welcoming. Most of the time, when he got a cold reception to a case he wanted to bring, he would take his superiors' word for it and lay off the case for a while. The Hunter Biden case was the first time he ever felt the need to press hard. The facts seemed so clear, and the case seemed like such an easy win, that he didn't see why the IRS would avoid trying to get it prosecuted.

Finally, he discussed the case with the supervisor who'd brought him into the international tax group, an agent we'll call Matt White, who agreed to look into the case further before sending it up for referral. Most of the time, Joe would have done this himself. In previous cases, when he noticed something strange on a bank report, he'd sent that report to the U.S. Attorney's Office and asked if someone in that office wanted to look into it. He figured he could do the same thing with the Hunter Biden case. Matt told him not to.

"You can't send it," he said. "That's a tax disclosure issue."

Here, we should probably provide a little context. At the IRS, where we both still work, we take taxpayer privacy very seriously. That's why you get a special PIN (usually in the mail) that only you know. It's why you have such a hard time logging onto the website, with all its buttons and login screens, all designed to ensure that no one other than you can access your tax information. That obsession with privacy extends to the criminal tax cases we work. From the beginning, Joe was taught the rules for transmitting the tax data to anyone outside the IRS building. Strict rules needed to be followed.

But for years now, Joe and his team had been identifying potential tax crimes and sending them up the chain for review. He'd never once heard serious concerns about disclosure issues. A few days after he first brought the Hunter Biden case to his team, one of his supervisors got a little closer to the truth. Leaning in over a conference table, this person said, "Listen, when you're dealing with a political family like this, you have to have more than just an allegation and evidence related to that allegation. In order for this case to move forward, you basically have to show a significant amount of evidence and similar wrongdoing in other areas."

In other words, Joe needed to show more than unfiled tax returns, unpaid tax debts, and testimony from divorce filings. He didn't agree. If anyone else in the country—especially someone bringing in the kind of money that Hunter Biden seemed to be bringing in—had failed to timely pay their taxes for 2015 and *also* failed to timely file their tax returns for 2016 and 2017, that person would have found themselves in serious trouble. But when it came to the Bidens, no one wanted to be the one to say anything. Joe got the sense that if he didn't continue to press the issue, it was possible that no one in federal law enforcement would ever pick it up again.

After a great deal of pushing and two failed attempts, Joe finally put together a third report on Hunter Biden that his supervisor deemed ready to be sent up to the Department of Justice's Tax Division for its approval on elevating the matter.

Unlike his previous two reports, this third one contained evidence that would elevate the potential charges from misdemeanors (not filing tax returns) to felonies (filing *false* tax returns). The evidence in these reports was complicated, and tax disclosure laws prevent us from going into too much detail. Suffice it to say that the case seemed ironclad to Joe and that the investigation should proceed like any other. The fact that his supervisors were finally letting his files leave the building seemed like the surest sign yet that the case would succeed.

Then, in early 2019, news came down from his superiors that surprised him. The FBI was also looking into Hunter Biden. While they weren't looking into his tax returns specifically (and we cannot disclose exactly *what* they were looking into here), the investigation overlapped enough that someone suggested combining the two investigations into one. This presented several problems for Joe. For one thing, the case he put together needed to be worked in Washington, D.C. The case the FBI was working needed to be worked in Delaware. Someone needed to win. And given that the IRS is the only agency designated by Congress to investigate tax crimes, the investigation couldn't proceed without Joe or someone else from the agency on the team.

What followed were a few tense negotiations regarding venue. Joe did what's known as a "venue analysis," making the case that the investigation needed to happen in Washington, D.C., where the IRS tax investigation was based. He discussed this issue several times with attorneys and IRS leadership to plead his case. During those presentations, he demonstrated voluminous knowledge of the facts. He also appeared headstrong about moving the case forward. There were good reasons for this. For one thing, Joe loved his job. Thoroughness was important to him, and so was the pursuit of justice. But he'd also been through a few things in his personal life that made burying himself in work seem like a good idea.

In the beginning of 2018, not long after he'd started his investigation into the social media company, Joe had been robbed at gunpoint while standing in his driveway. Three men had come out of nowhere shortly after seven o'clock in the morning, just as Joe was leaving the house for work. They'd taken his wallet, his phone, and both a personal car and his government-owned vehicle, along with everything that was inside them. He'd lost Christmas presents and his work bag. One of the only things the thieves left him with were his badge and gun, which he'd decided to keep holstered for fear that he was greatly outnumbered. Shortly before being issued his firearm, Joe had passed a basic training course, but that course hadn't included a scenario in which he was accosted by three men with guns, so he decided to take cover instead of shooting from the hip. This snap decision had probably kept him alive. But it had also left him in fear that the guys were going to come back. (It later turned out that the MO of these guys was to steal cars, then come back to the house a few weeks later with the keys for everything else.)

At the time, Joe had been dating a guy who worked as a personal trainer. We'll call him David. The robbery freaked David out so much that he offered to have Joe move in with him. That was nice, but it was stressful. Around the same time, he found out that his father had been diagnosed with a rare type of liver cancer that gave him less than one year to live. This meant that he was going to have to take several trips back to his hometown of Cleveland, Ohio, to care for his dad. So, given the circumstances, it was understandable that he'd want to focus all his energy on work, ensuring that every case he put together would result in a conviction. It was the only way he knew how to keep sane.

In the end, Joe lost the battle over venue selection. It was determined that the FBI's Hunter Biden case, which was now joined with the one Joe had started the previous year, would be worked from Delaware, not Washington. This presented one serious problem, although not one that anyone in the leadership of the IRS, DOJ, or FBI seemed to care about. We've already said that in almost every respect, Hunter Biden was a normal citizen, and he should be treated like one. He'd failed to timely file his taxes, and in one instance, he had appeared to file a false return. He needed to be investigated just like anyone else. In Washington, that was almost possible. In Delaware, the place Joe Biden and his family had called home for more than seven decades, it was not. Even before the case went to Biden's home state (where he'd served as a senator for many years before becoming Barack Obama's vice president), Joe had heard rumors that Biden often popped in at the local FBI office, just to speak with the agents in the office. Biden knew everyone in local politics, and he'd interacted at least once with most top law enforcement officials in the state. To Joe, investigating a member of the Biden family in Delaware would have been like investigating Beyoncé in a gay bar. Even if you got things off the ground, you could be sure that just about everyone you spoke to would not want you to succeed.

But the decision had come down. For the next few months, Joe tried to work with the members of the investigative unit: two FBI agents, two forensic accountants, two lawyers from the Tax Division, two assistant United States attorneys from Delaware, and him. In the beginning, this involved a great deal of travel between his office and the various government office buildings where these people worked. Because of the sensitive nature of the case, all the work was covert. Nothing could leak to the press, and nothing could be discussed with colleagues who weren't involved in the case. This meant that Joe often found himself closed off from his fellow IRS agents in a way he hadn't been before, especially those in leadership positions who hadn't wanted the Hunter Biden case to go forward.

Rather than dealing with the awkwardness head-on, he spent most of the time he wasn't working on rebuilding his shattered personal life and tending to his father, whose relationship with Joe had always been complicated, to say the least. He also found himself reading a great deal about the case he was working on—not just financial documents and bank statements but ancillary reports in newspapers, magazines, and even books. If Joe was going to spend so much of his time at work trying to bring someone to justice, it seemed only fair that he make some attempt to understand that person and why he'd acted in the way he had. He figured he might find a few redeeming qualities about Hunter Biden if he looked hard enough.

No matter how hard he looked, though, nothing materialized.

If anything, the opposite happened.

―

Today, it's hard to remember a time before Joe Biden was president, or even a serious *candidate* for president. But at the very beginning of 2019, that was exactly the situation we found ourselves in. Most political commentators, certainly the ones Joe and his friends kept up with, said that Biden was far too old and over the hill to win the Democratic Party's nomination. The MSNBC crowd was sure we'd have someone like Elizabeth Warren or Bernie Sanders on the ballot next November.

"Many in the Democratic establishment worry that Biden's time has passed," according to an article in *Politico* published around this time, "and that the party needs a fresher face to take on Trump." On Twitter, the notion that a president who'd be over eighty years old at the end of a potential first term was a joke. Almost no one took it seriously.

One place Joe Biden *was* still taken seriously, though, was Delaware—specifically in the city of Wilmington, where he'd lived for just under eight decades. There, the Biden family was a local institution. Everyone in town knew their story. Over time, Joe got to know it, too. At night, when he came back from the office, he'd sit up reading books and magazine articles about the Bidens, trying to get a sense of the people he was investigating. At first, the research didn't turn up anything that wasn't common knowledge.

Joe Biden, who'd spent most of his childhood in Scranton, Pennsylvania, where his father was a car salesman, had come to Delaware at the age of ten, working his way up through the state's political machine to become the youngest candidate for the United States Senate in American history. Interestingly, he'd only been allowed to take office due to a slight quirk in the United States Constitution. Although Joe Biden was only twenty-nine years old when he was elected (one year below the constitutionally mandated minimum age for senators), he turned thirty on November 20, 1972, slipping in just under the wire. For a while, he failed to distinguish himself in any meaningful way, mostly toeing the Democratic Party's line on the issues of the day.

Most in-depth magazine profiles mentioned Biden's affinity for Amtrak trains. Unlike other senators, who maintained two residences and flew into Washington for about five days at a time, Senator Biden commuted back and forth to his home in Wilmington, Delaware, every weekday. His colleagues told stories about sitting with Biden in afternoon meetings, preparing to dive into a long discussion of a particular bill, only to have him slam his hands on the table so he could make the last evening train home. In other words, the man almost never stayed out of Delaware for longer than a single workday.

Along with this run-of-the-mill biographical stuff, Joe also read the full story of the car accident that took the lives of Joe Biden's first wife and his one-year-old daughter, Naomi. The details were brutal. It was almost impossible not to feel some sympathy for Hunter, who survived the accident along with his older brother, Beau. For the next two decades, according to most reports, Hunter lived in his brother's shadow, always feeling inferior to a person described as "the spitting image of his father," and "a great guy." Unlike Hunter, Beau became a soldier, then he returned home to serve as Delaware's attorney general, earning a reputation as a principled prosecutor with aspirations for higher office.

Hunter, meanwhile, struggled with addiction, got a law degree, and relied mostly on his father's name to make a living. In the summer of 2006, according to a report about the Biden family in *Politico*, Hunter joined forces with his uncle James Biden to found an investment fund called Paradigm. One executive who was quoted in the article stated that during an early meeting, "James Biden made it clear that he viewed the fund as a way to take money from rich foreigners who could not legally give money to his older brother or his campaign account." The executive remembers James Biden saying, "We've got investors lined up in a line of 747s filled with cash ready to invest in this company." Hunter Biden joined this investment firm despite having no experience in finance or the kinds of complex legal transactions that the firm would be doing. He seemed to have been hired, as he would be dozens of times throughout his life, because his last name was "Biden."

What really caught Joe's eye was a report detailing an outside audit of the company, conducted in July 2008 by the firm Briggs, Bunting & Dougherty. According to a report produced by the auditing firm, Paradigm showed "a failure to reconcile Investment Advisors reimbursement of fund expenses, failure to reconcile and review cash account on a timely basis, and failure to reconcile and review various other accounts on a timely basis." This didn't have any connection to Hunter Biden's failure to file taxes for 2015 and 2016, but it did serve as evidence that his financial troubles began long before Joe came across his name on those bank reports in November 2018.

From there, it only seemed to get worse. Digging into the story about the divorce filings, Joe found mentions of a strange diamond that Hunter Biden had been given on a trip to Miami in May 2017. Further research revealed that it had been given to Hunter after a meeting with a Chinese energy tycoon named Ye Jianming. Hunter and Ye had been meeting about a potential business venture. Asked by a reporter from *The New Yorker* whether he believed the diamond constituted a bribe, Hunter said, "What would they be bribing me for? My dad wasn't in office." Hunter's ex-wife believed the diamond was worth at least $80,000; Hunter said it was worth only $10,000.

There were other threads to pull on. For instance, in April 2014, Hunter Biden joined the board of Burisma Holdings, a Ukrainian energy company looking to make connections with the West. Despite having no experience in energy policy or corporate governance, Hunter was said to be paid about $50,000 per month to attend board meetings and conferences in Europe once or twice a year. Alan Apter, who was chairman of the board at the time, noted in a press release that the appointment was "totally based on merit." Things got very shady when Joe Biden, who oversaw Ukraine as part of his portfolio in the Obama White House, took a trip to Ukraine as vice president in December 2015.

During this trip, according to reporting by mostly right-wing media, Vice President Biden had pressured the Ukrainian government to fire a prosecutor named Viktor Shokin, largely believed to be corrupt by the Obama administration. It worked. Years later, rumors would swirl about whether Shokin had plans to investigate Burisma and its board, including Hunter Biden. At the time Joe was looking into these things, however, these were only rumors, mostly published on news sites that seemed to have a negative view of the Bidens no matter what. He didn't know what was true and what was propaganda.

In the end, his little research excursion into the Biden family yielded more questions than answers. He didn't find out whether Hunter Biden had broken lobbying laws or engaged in serious breaches of ethics with his conduct, though it certainly appeared that way. All Joe knew was what he'd seen in Hunter Biden's bank reports, and what he'd seen in his bank reports clearly indicated that Hunter had probably committed serious tax violations. If nothing else, he had failed to timely file his taxes, which was a misdemeanor tax offense worth a thorough investigation. He figured that most of the things he didn't yet know probably weren't relevant to the case. Either way, the only way to learn them was by sticking with the investigation he'd started and making sure it was carried out correctly and efficiently.

What Joe didn't know, and *couldn't* have known during those first few months, was that the answers to every question he had about the Hunter Biden case—and many answers to questions he hadn't even thought to ask yet—were sitting on a silver MacBook Pro that Hunter had used for years. This laptop, which had finally broken down after being used for explicit webcamming, corrupt dealmaking, and angry email-sending, was not in the possession of the IRS or the FBI (yet). At the time Joe was taking his first steps into the investigation that would ultimately lead to serious charges for Hunter Biden, it wasn't even in *Hunter's* possession anymore.

It was, rather, sitting in the back room of a small computer repair shop in Delaware, where a man named Mac Isaac was attempting to get it up and running again. Soon, he'd come across evidence that would turn Joe's investigation from a small tax issue into a case that had the potential to bring down the entire Biden crime family.

TWO

WAITING (AND WAITING, AND WAITING...)

BY THE TIME Gary Shapley took over the International Tax and Financial Crimes Unit at the IRS in late 2019, he'd seen a lot.

After interning at the Department of Defense after college, he'd done a two-year stint at the office of the NSA's inspector general. When things went wrong inside the NSA—when there were allegations of corruption, malfeasance, or stonewalling among the spies and analysts who worked there—it fell to the inspector general to conduct a full investigation. Although much of what Gary saw is classified, we can say that he learned a great deal about what people in large organizations will do to protect one another, especially when the stakes are high.

After the NSA, Gary went straight to the IRS, where he'd been for almost twelve years on the afternoon he met Joe Ziegler. All morning, he'd been meeting people on the new team he'd be leading. They had done team-building exercises, but Gary hadn't been able to speak to anyone in much depth. Now he sat in the corner of the conference room, listening while people carried on conversations about things he didn't know much about. The supervisor in charge hadn't introduced him. He was speaking about what they'd be doing for the rest of the day: a tour around the monuments, lunch, then a few other team-building exercises.

Joe raised his hand, cutting off the speech.

"So . . . I mean, sorry," he said. "But who's this guy sitting in the corner?"

Every pair of eyes in the room—all ten of them—turned to Gary. They all seemed to know that he was the new leader of their group and that he'd replaced Matt White, who wasn't exactly well-liked. But no one had said anything.

Joe had.

This, as Gary would learn, was something he did often. If there was something everyone wanted to say that no one was quite willing to say—that there was, for instance, something deeply wrong with the way leadership was handling a particular case—Joe would say it. And he'd do it in a way that was charming.

"Sorry," said the person leading the session, also turning around. "This is Gary Shapley. He's our new—"

"He's going to be our new team leader, right?" Joe said.

Some people laughed. Others shifted nervously in their chairs. Gary got up and ran through his resume quickly. He let the team know he was excited to get to work with them. He and Joe shared a quick look as he sat back down. Right away, Gary could tell he was probably a good agent. He seemed well-liked by everyone in the room. But he also looked a little strung out, like something had been weighing heavily on him.

About an hour later, Gary found out what it was.

"There's this case," Joe said. "It's just . . . I mean, it's like nothing I've ever worked on before."

We were walking slightly ahead of our group in front of the Lincoln Memorial. A few team members snapped pictures. Tourists streamed by in thick jackets, pausing for a moment to glance up at the enormous stone statue of our sixteenth president.

"How do you mean?" Gary asked.

"Well, it's Hunter Biden."

Gary said nothing, letting his eyes go wide and reveal the surprise he felt.

"I know, right? It's, like, *that* Hunter Biden. Turns out the guy hasn't paid his taxes in years. I was reviewing these bank reports, and it turns out he's been spending hundreds of thousands of dollars on hookers, cars, college tuition. Pretty much everything but paying his taxes."

"Huh."

"It appears to be an open and shut case worthy of a thorough investigation. If it were anyone else, I would have interviewed him already. But . . . I don't know, *something* is going on with this one."

We kept walking, heading for another monument. The dome of the Capitol building loomed in the distance. No matter how many times he walked past it on his way to work, the sight of all these monuments, especially the Capitol, had never failed to make Joe pause and feel a little awe. The United States government, he knew, stood up for all Americans equally. As an investigator at the IRS, he was proud to be part of that.

"First, they told me not to do it. Then they said I could do it, but I needed to have 'all my ducks in a row.' Then they said that when you're dealing with a political family, you can't treat them like everyone else."

And on and on it went.

By the time they finished the tour of the monuments, Joe had barely scratched the surface of all the stonewalling he'd experienced. Eventually, they moved on to other things. He found that Gary was an easy guy to talk to, and he seemed to share the same philosophy about law enforcement that Joe did. Gary seemed thorough, and he did business with an air of impartiality. He cared about doing the job well. Everything else was secondary. For once, it was good to be speaking with someone who didn't believe bringing this case was a bad political move. It was, in fact, good to be speaking to *anyone* in the building without layers of tense awkwardness running underneath the conversation.

Gary, meanwhile, was laser focused on only one thing. He wanted to make sure that the Hunter Biden investigation was opened one hundred percent—no, one *thousand* percent—by the book. There could be no appearance of impropriety or political bias. Every move that Joe and his colleagues had made needed to be completely by the book. Gary knew that someday this case would be picked apart by journalists, political operatives, and private citizens. If anyone had made a single mistake, it was going to come to light. He wanted to know about these mistakes early so he could get ahead of them. If there was anything to find—a stray email about how someone didn't like Joe Biden, for instance, or an agent who'd worn a MAGA hat to even a single meeting—Gary wanted to find it.

Luckily, there wasn't. Gary was happy to find after that long first session that Joe had conducted himself flawlessly. He'd noticed all the right things, notated them in exactly the right ways, and kept clear records of it all. If it weren't still covert and completely secret, Gary would have used Joe's Hunter Biden case file to teach new recruits to the Criminal Investigation Division how to begin opening their own investigations. Of course, it *was* still top secret, even to most agents in the building. For almost two years, Joe had been working the case on his own, traveling to meet with his counterparts at the FBI only a few times a week. In the building, though, he was isolated, especially from leadership. Gary had never been an expert in office politics (he preferred to keep his head down and work), but even he could see that something was going on between the higher-ups at the IRS and Joe Ziegler.

At first, he wondered if it was political in the more common sense of the word. On the one hand, you had an IRS special agent working on a case about the son of a former vice president—whose father, in defiance of pretty much all expectations, was now the front-runner for the Democratic nomination again. On the other hand, you had a group of people (the leadership of the IRS) who tended to lean left politically. Maybe the top brass at the IRS was worried they had some kind of secret Republican sleeper agent on their hands, a guy who was hungry to take down the Biden family to pave the way for a second Trump term no matter what the cost. It took about three-and-a-half seconds of speaking to Joe Zeigler for Gary to realize that this probably wasn't the case. Whenever the conversation did veer around to politics, which it almost never did, Joe was always hesitant to express his opinion. When he did, it was usually mild and based on a left-leaning outlook on the world. If Gary had to guess how Joe got his news, he'd have said Twitter and a few minutes of MSNBC at the gym.

This was a good thing. Over the years, Gary had learned that when you work in federal law enforcement, staying apolitical was generally the best course of action. As a result, he was careful never to post political messages online (not that this took much effort). He didn't donate to political candidates, and he didn't own any clothing with political slogans or the names of candidates on it. Over the years, he'd voted for candidates with both "R" and "D" in front of their names. Once, when his children expressed an interest in seeing how elections are run in the United States, he'd taken them to the local polling location to vote in a midterm. Other than that, he'd only ever cast votes in the general, along with about 60 percent of other Americans.

As the conversation continued, Gary got the sense that Joe had experienced more than a few bumps in the road during the early months of the Hunter Biden investigation. Some of these he heard about directly, others were only hinted at. Finally, just a few days after he finally took over the group, he had Joe sit down and tell him exactly what had happened since the case was joined with the FBI's investigation in Delaware. By this point, the case had been given a name, and that name was "Sportsman."

For anyone wondering what the word *sportsman* has to do with the Biden family, the answer is nothing. Whenever the FBI opens an investigation, that investigation is assigned a name by the case agent. The initial investigation into Donald Trump's alleged collusion with Russia, for instance, was called Crossfire Hurricane, a phrase that had only ever appeared in the song "Jumpin' Jack Flash" by The Rolling Stones. An ancillary investigation was called Crossfire Razor. Other interesting names from history include Midyear Exam, the Clinton email probe; Encore, a Russia-related inquiry into Michael Flynn; Ghost Stories, the FBI's case against Russian sleeper agents; and Trojan Shield, a sting operation where the FBI secretly ran a criminal encrypted messaging app.

The strange name was just one of the many ways that the Delaware FBI office had changed the Hunter Biden investigation. There had also been stonewalling, slow-walking, and deliberate confusion at every step of the way. Gary was no stranger to the little tensions that can emerge when two agencies work together on a complex case. He'd spent a great deal of time working for the Department of Justice's tax division himself. But this was different. This seemed deliberate, and it seemed to be coming right from the top. These suspicions (and that's all they were at first) were confirmed with almost every meeting we had.

Finally, after noticing enough irregularities to confirm his suspicions, Gary asked Joe a flat-out question.

"What the hell has been going on with this case?"

Joe tried his best to give Gary a straight answer. But given all the examples of bureaucratic meddling that came readily to mind, that wasn't easy. Instead, he launched into a two-hour tirade, complete with visual aids and more than a few obscene hand gestures, detailing all that he'd endured between November 2018 and the end of 2019, when Gary took over. What follows is a cleaned-up, far less profane version of that tirade.

—

"We can't do that."

Joe was in a meeting with his counterparts at the DOJ. It was the summer of 2019, about six months before Gary took over the International Tax and Financial Crimes Unit. Matt White, his current supervisor, was not in the room. Neither were any of his colleagues from IRS headquarters. Instead, he was here in Delaware with the small team that had gathered around the Hunter Biden case: two FBI agents, four attorneys, one forensic accountant, and himself. He was being told, not for the first time, that under no circumstances could this investigation "go overt."

We should explain.

In the beginning, all criminal tax investigations are designated as "covert." The special agent in charge of the case does not call up the person being investigated and let them know they might be in trouble. There are a few reasons for this, chief among them that we want to make sure we're correct about the potential tax crimes this person may have committed. Nothing ruins an afternoon like being notified by the IRS that you're under suspicion of tax fraud only to find out days later that you've done nothing wrong. To that end, several people look at the bank statements and ancillary documents under review, just to make sure the special agent who reviewed those documents first did everything correctly. Under normal circumstances, this review process takes no more than a few days or weeks.

But these were not normal circumstances.

By the time he was told for the tenth time that he could not go overt with the investigation, Joe had been working on the Hunter Biden case for roughly six months. It had been more than thirty days since his supervisors allowed him to elevate the case to DOJ Tax for review. That number, *thirty*, is important. According to the Internal Revenue Manual, or "IRM," the special agent in charge of a case *must* reach out and interview the subject of his or her investigation within thirty days of that case being elevated to DOJ Tax. If the special agent does *not* reach out to his subject for an interview within thirty days, he or she is required to write a report detailing the reasons why. Several times, Joe had requested to comply with standard procedure and schedule an interview with Hunter Biden.

For one thing, this would have put Hunter on notice. It also would have ensured that any steps Hunter took *after* the interview would automatically have become part of the case. Again, if this had been any other taxpayer, this is exactly what Joe and the team would have done. But it wasn't any other taxpayer. It was a member of an extremely powerful political family—one that seemed to be able to intimidate veteran prosecutors without even doing anything. Time and again, when Joe requested to interview Hunter Biden, prosecutors from the U.S. Attorney's Office in Delaware told him it wasn't a good idea. The reason they finally gave was that the evidence in the case needed to be preserved for a potential future investigation by the FBI, something that didn't quite make sense to Joe.

But he wasn't in charge. He was only one member of a team, and that team had to answer to prosecutors. For a while, one of these prosecutors was an ex-military guy named Jamie McCall. A hard-hitting go-getter with a demonstrated ability to close tough cases, Jamie was exactly the kind of assistant U.S. attorney Joe had been hoping would get the case. In the early stages of the investigation, Jamie and Joe worked hand-in-glove, taking all the right steps and moving things forward. He'd been a judge advocate in the Marine Corps, and it showed. Still, he couldn't seem to convince anyone that it was time to go overt and take real action.

The best they could do for the moment was to draft electronic search warrants, which would allow them to search digital records pertaining to the case. This meant potential emails, text messages, and financial reports that were directly linked to the case. As you might expect, these documents needed to be written with extreme care to ensure access to all needed materials.

By the summer of 2019, the first electronic search warrant was all set to go. Joe had done all the necessary legwork, and he'd written the warrant with rigorous attention to detail. In the months he spent working on the investigation, he became quite close with the team working the case. They shared details about their personal lives, and they developed an easy rapport during meetings and long research sessions. By the time they sent the first electronic search warrants up to a magistrate judge for approval, they were friends, which is not an uncommon occurrence on teams who work closely together for long periods of time. After a while, even the frequent setbacks became opportunities for team bonding.

And in that sense, there was a *lot* of team bonding.

Consider that in the summer of 2019, the magistrate judge in charge of signing the first electronic warrant in the case—a job that should have taken all of three seconds—made an inappropriate remark while touching her pen to the paper. Due to a law known as the exclusionary rule, this meant that the warrant she'd just signed was no longer valid. Joe and the team would have to spend the next four months doing everything they'd just done over again, writing yet another search warrant based on the information they were now collecting for a second time. This was frustrating, to say the least.

It was even more frustrating because in the summer of 2019, the leadership of the FBI in Delaware began to get far more involved in the case than they'd been before. Suddenly, the top brass in the bureau wanted to be kept abreast of everything the team was doing. During one memorable meeting in 2019, the team learned that Joe Biden himself was coming into the office with the intention of discussing a personal issue with the leadership of the FBI. By this point, he had announced his presidential run. Having a presidential candidate stop by the offices of their local FBI field office might seem strange to most people. But in Delaware, this kind of thing was perfectly normal.

During the early stages of the investigation, Joe had heard about something called the "Delaware Way." A common phrase around Joe and Hunter's home state, this phrase referred to the way local politicians protected their own, operated behind closed doors, and ensured that power and influence remained concentrated among a select few insiders. Deals were often made quietly, favors exchanged, and accountability sidestepped in the name of maintaining political and business relationships. Examples included former Delaware governor Jack Markell, who was known for his close ties to corporate interests, particularly in the financial services industry, and for policies that benefited major employers while often sidestepping broader transparency measures. Another example was Senator Tom Carper, who built a long career in Delaware politics by maintaining strong relationships with both party insiders and business leaders, ensuring that regulatory scrutiny rarely disrupted the status quo.

By all accounts, Joe Biden and his extended family had long been proponents of the "Delaware Way," yet another reason that the local FBI office was probably not the best place to run an investigation of that family. In 1972, Biden had been accused of leveraging his political connections to secure a lucrative real estate deal involving a former DuPont estate, raising allegations of favoritism and insider dealing. The property, a sprawling mansion in Greenville, Delaware, was in disrepair and slated for demolition, but Biden—despite his modest senator's salary—somehow managed to acquire it at a steep discount. Critics have long pointed to this as an early example of how Biden used his political standing to enrich himself while maintaining the carefully crafted image of an "average Joe."

In 2019, his brother James Biden—Hunter's uncle—had been accused of using the Biden name to secure a major investment deal in the healthcare sector, despite having no relevant experience. James was involved in a scheme to purchase struggling rural hospitals, allegedly promising potential investors that his family connections would open doors to Middle Eastern financing and government contracts. The deal collapsed, leaving unpaid debts and lawsuits in its wake, but James Biden walked away unscathed—just another example of how the Biden name shielded family members from real consequences.

These scandals, however, had not kept Joe Biden from power. They also hadn't damaged the relationship between his family and local law enforcement, evidenced by the way he was able to walk in and out of the FBI field office seemingly at will. Aside from the metaphorical coziness, the Biden compound was *literally* close by. Every time Joe attended a meeting about the Hunter Biden case in Delaware, he did so knowing that Joe Biden lived less than two miles from the place he attended meetings. Walking into the building, it was hard not to feel like a complete outsider. Even the people on his team, who had by this point become relatively good friends, mostly lived and worked in Delaware. They were used to the easy, almost painfully slow speed of politics in the state.

Throughout all of 2019, Joe had been amazed at how slowly the Delaware U.S. Attorney's Office had moved on the Biden case. He wasn't sure whether this was because they were a tiny office without very much experience on high-level cases, or they really didn't want the Biden case to go forward quickly. As the presidential primaries wore on, though, he began to get answers. Every time he suggested moving forward on an aspect of the case that might implicate Joe Biden—or even one that could implicate someone close to Joe Biden, such as his son—Joe Ziegler was told that it probably wasn't a good idea. By this point, Joe Biden had yet to win a single presidential primary. He was only the former vice president of the United States, mounting a campaign against President Trump just like nearly a dozen other Democrats were doing at the time. And the investigation, it bears mentioning, was not about Joe Biden; it was about *his son*.

Still, the stonewalling continued. So did the odd looks and strange insinuations from IRS leadership. Sometimes, these insinuations were delivered to the entire Hunter Biden investigative team via email from Matt White, who was still Joe's direct superior at the time. At least once a month, sometimes more, Matt would write an email that contained a link to news coverage about the Biden family. When there were developments about Hunter Biden in the public eye, Matt always sent links to the full investigative team.

Now, we should note that by itself, the act of sending links is perfectly fine. People do it all the time. But Matt would often write his own commentary below these links, making the case that the investigation into Hunter Biden might violate either his Fourth Amendment or Sixth Amendment rights. No matter what specific laws Matt cited—and there were many—the general thrust of his mass emails was always the same.

This investigation is a bad idea, he seemed to say, not wanting to cross the line into giving an outright order. *Please drop it.*

Joe asked him to stop sending the emails to the full team multiple times. He had no problem with Matt sending *him* updates on the case, but getting such a flurry of strange commentary every few days was beginning to spook the people he was working with. Eventually, he had to go over Matt's head and talk to his supervisor about it. But that only happened *after* Matt had sent a ton of articles, some of which included Twitter posts from President Trump.

Finally, after repeating legwork they'd already done, Joe and the team sent up yet another email search warrant for approval by a different magistrate judge. This time it was signed and executed without much trouble. As soon as the warrant was executed, the team had troves of emails, text messages, and memos involving

Hunter Biden, all pulled straight from his email account. This was exhilarating. But it was also overwhelming. After so many months of sitting around with nothing much to look at other than bank reports and news articles, Joe and the team had piles of stuff to review.

Slowly, they made their case, cross-referencing emails with financial statements and trying to paint an accurate picture of Hunter Biden's overseas business activities. It didn't take long for this picture to get very dark. Right away, they noticed payments for drugs, prostitutes, and other seedy items, paid from Hunter's corporate account. They also noticed frequent conversations regarding business schemes that hadn't yet been reported in the media—schemes where the people involved used first initials and strange aliases. Hunter Biden was fond of yelling at people during messages about these schemes, threatening to use his influence (or, rather, his father's influence) to punish people if his exact needs weren't fulfilled.

Joe Biden's name came up frequently, though it was always cloaked in some kind of alias. Although this was interesting at the time, it wasn't what Joe had opened the investigation to look at. He didn't care about the internal dynamics of the Biden family. As time went on, though, he came to realize that what he *was* interested in investigating—namely Hunter Biden's shady and potentially illegal business practices—seemed to be inextricable from the Biden family dynamics. As they reviewed the emails and texts that came in as a result of the search warrant, Joe and the team came to understand that they weren't dealing with just one wayward fifty-something-year-old kid with a drug problem and bad financial habits.

They were dealing with a crime family.

It made sense. Over the years, there had been plenty of allegations against Joe Biden, his brother Jim, and Hunter. None of these had ever quite stuck—probably, Joe thought, as a result of Delaware's cozy political culture, as well as Joe Biden's almost preternatural ability to brush scandals off his back—but Joe still got the feeling that there was more to see behind the scenes. As he continued combing through the evidence he had (which, in the end, would turn out to be only the tip of the iceberg), he found himself pulled into something much larger than an investigation into unfiled tax returns and unpaid taxes.

There were holes, though. Email chains terminated without explanation. Many days of data were missing. There was enough to make the criminal tax case, to be sure, but not without interviewing Hunter Biden and members of his family. Joe and the team were all set to write up their findings and begin conducting in-person interviews when a notice came in from an FBI field office in Albuquerque, New Mexico, of all places. An agent there had received word from a man named Mac Isaac, who claimed to have a laptop belonging to Hunter Biden in his possession. At first, Joe wasn't sure why this would matter. Then he dug into the statement that Mac Isaac had given to the FBI when he reported the existence of the laptop. This device, which was confirmed as belonging to Hunter Biden on November 6, 2019, contained thousands of photos, emails, texts, and documents. It also probably contained the answers to every question Joe and his team had been asking since the start of the investigation.

On December 3, a little over a week before the Baltimore Field Office of the FBI would take possession of the laptop and an accompanying external hard drive, Joe drafted a search warrant affidavit. If accepted, this would allow him to search the laptop for any material related to the case. As usual, things moved slowly. He sent it up the chain as soon as he finished drafting it, and then he waited.

And waited.

In the meantime, Joe Biden was picking up a little steam in the presidential race—enough that *Axios* sat for a one-on-one interview with him that was published on December 8. Over the course of that interview, which focused mostly on what Biden planned to do for the country, Hunter Biden's work with the Ukrainian oil company Burisma came up. Joe Biden, whose purview in the Obama White House had included "Ukrainian affairs," among other things, said he had no idea what his son was doing on the board of the energy company. By this point, Joe didn't yet have hard proof that this was a lie. But he'd seen enough emails shooting back and forth between members of the Biden family to know that it probably wasn't likely. In that family, nothing stayed secret. Everyone seemed to know exactly what everyone else was doing at all times.

On December 13, Joe obtained a Title 26 search warrant for the contents of Hunter Biden's laptop. Title 26 refers to the section of U.S. law governing federal tax crimes, giving investigators the authority to seize and review evidence related to tax violations. The warrant allowed Joe to examine the laptop's contents for potential tax fraud, including financial records, emails, and business transactions that could indicate unreported income or improper deductions. However, the scope of the warrant was limited to tax-related offenses—meaning that while investigators might uncover other potential crimes, such as foreign lobbying violations or money laundering, they could only pursue them if they had a direct connection to Hunter's tax filings.

WAITING (AND WAITING, AND WAITING . . .)   43

Of course, Joe wasn't just going to have the laptop delivered to his desk so he could start poking around on it. That's not the way we handle things. Instead, he had to wait for a specialized group of experts on the FBI's computer analysis and response team to comb through the contents of the laptop, organize them, and make them available for review. This meant more waiting.

And then some more waiting.

In the meantime, Joe continued to push to go overt. Even without the evidence from the laptop, they had more than enough evidence to interview Hunter Biden and move forward with the case. But the resistance from leadership continued, and it only intensified as Joe Biden got closer to winning the Democratic Party's nomination.

Whenever Joe sent something up the chain for approval, the attorneys from the DOJ would insist he wait.

And wait some more.

By January 2020, when Gary took over as the supervisor of the Hunter Biden investigation, it had been just over a year since Joe first noticed Hunter's name on bank records related to his online social media case.

Any other investigation could have been closed months earlier.

In general, the IRS strives to resolve all criminal tax cases within about a year, maybe eighteen months if things are extremely complicated. That's part of the reason we have a requirement that agents go out and interview the target of an investigation within thirty days. Among other things, it ensures that cases move quickly and that people don't have investigations looming over their heads for years at a time.

But when it came to the Biden case, everyone was just fine with the delays. In fact, Gary noticed right away that leadership across the board—from the IRS and the DOJ to the various people at the FBI who now seemed extremely interested in the Biden case—seemed to *enjoy* the delays. No one wanted to move forward. Around this time, Gary heard the first rumblings from people that they should probably wait until after the 2020 election to make any serious moves in this case. It wouldn't be proper, they said, to do otherwise.

There were other setbacks. In early 2020, Jamie McCall, the hard-charging prosecutor who'd been one of Joe's only real allies on the case, left the U.S. Attorney's Office to work in private practice. This left another assistant United States attorney, a woman named Lesley Wolf, in charge of the investigation. Gary hadn't worked with Lesley before. He had no reason to believe she'd try to tank the investigation. But given Joe's account of what had transpired on the case in 2019, he wasn't hopeful that anything would get done soon.

Still, he continued working the case, along with about a dozen others he was now overseeing. In March, he heard from Joe and the team that their review of the materials on Hunter Biden's laptop was complete. He and Joe often reviewed the evidence together, and they were both shocked by what they saw. Although they were only reviewing materials related to tax fraud, that still meant plenty of salacious material. Now, with Joe Biden winning primaries left and right on his way to becoming the Democratic nominee for president, Gary knew they had more than enough to go overt on the case.

The next step was to get physical. Rather than poring over documents in the office, they would send agents to serve search warrants at Hunter Biden's home, where there were mountains of evidence, as well as a storage unit that contained everything from Hunter's law office. On March 6, Gary sent a "significant case report" up the chain of command. Within the IRS, significant case reports are formal updates used to brief senior leadership on major developments in high-profile or complex investigations. They outline investigative progress, proposed next steps, and any potential risks or obstacles requiring attention or approval from upper management. In that report, he notified IRS leadership that Joe and the "Sportsman" team would be ready to seek physical search warrants in California, Arkansas, New York, and Washington, D.C., by the middle of that month.

On that day, the disease that would come to be known as Covid-19 was still mostly contained to China. Almost no one in the United States knew that cases were beginning to spread to major metropolitan hubs. We were still going into the office every day, working our cases and filing our paperwork as usual. And the leadership of the IRS, the DOJ, and the FBI, which had been looking for a good excuse to kick the Hunter Biden case down the road since it opened, still insisted that the team wait before going overt.

Then, in the middle of March, they got the excuse they'd been looking for.

After days of rising case counts and a few deaths in the United States from Covid-19, President Trump appeared in the White House briefing room with Dr. Anthony Fauci and a team of policy experts to announce the "15 Days to Slow the Spread" policy. The name seemed self-explanatory. Offices across the country, including the large IRS headquarters building in Washington, D.C., would close for just over two weeks. By then, it was expected that the "curve" would be flattened. Case counts would go back down, and everyone would be able to get back to work.

We were both unnerved by the two-week delay. Finally, we were on the verge of working this case in person, and all in-person activities were shut down. It seemed like yet another sign from the universe that this was going to be difficult. On the personal side of things, Joe worried about his father, whose health was already compromised. All the reporting he'd seen about Covid-19 indicated that it was particularly deadly to the elderly and those with underlying health conditions. He thought about putting his work aside and traveling back home, but flights were all temporarily grounded. Gary was similarly concerned about the vulnerable people in his life. But he figured they were dealing with a disease that might stick around for a week or two and then disappear.

He was wrong.

THREE

MISSING RETURNS

UNLIKE OUR INVESTIGATION, the presidential election kept moving forward during the early weeks of the pandemic. Joe Biden, who'd positioned himself as a moderate in the vein of Bill Clinton, was picking up steam. On April 8, Joe learned via a news alert that Bernie Sanders had dropped out of the presidential race, clearing the way for Biden to become the Democratic Party's presumptive nominee.

Joe knew this meant trouble.

Still, it was better to get the news from a *New York Times* alert than it was to get it from one of Matt White's foaming-at-the-mouth mass emails. Joe clicked on the alert and read the first few lines of the story—*"Bernie Sanders, the standard-bearer of the American left, ends his presidential campaign."* Then he lowered his phone, logged back into Zoom, and prepared for a meeting.

There was a lot of this in April 2020. You probably remember. Days would begin with short walks around the house and end with two (or three, or ten) episodes of a show on Netflix. In Gary's household, that meant *Young Sheldon*, a favorite of his kids. For Joe and David, it was *Tiger King.* In between, there were meetings on teleconferencing platforms that no one seemed quite sure how to work. People spoke when they were muted, they did embarrassing things when they thought their cameras were off, and they fell way behind on their work. For a bureaucracy that had been intentionally dragging its feet on an investigation, Covid-19 was a dream. Suddenly, emails about the Hunter Biden case didn't get returned because emails about *all* cases were slowing down. Supervisors had a lot on their plates, and everyone was trying to cope with having to do their jobs from home. The emails that did get returned usually began with something like, "I hope you're well in these challenging times" and then went on for a few hundred words about nothing.

Still, we pushed forward. A few months after we learned that the Hunter Biden laptop existed, the team was allowed to view a small selection of materials recovered from it. It wasn't what we wanted. But it was still interesting. Among the recovered messages were records of tense negotiations between Hunter Biden and James Biden, as well as representatives of several Chinese conglomerates with whom they were involved.

It was enough to make us extremely curious about what else was on the computer. On March 31, Gary wrote an email to Lesley Wolf noting that the team hadn't been allowed to see most of what Hunter Biden's laptop contained. Instead, we were looking over the scraps that had been handed down to us by DOJ leadership.

In practical terms, we weren't even looking at the full contents of the laptop. We were looking at digital "snapshots" of the computer that showed what it looked like at a certain point in time. These digital snapshots are called forensic images. They were created by the digital forensics team at the FBI and then sent over to us. A forensic image is a bit-for-bit copy of a device's entire storage—not just the visible files but also deleted items, metadata, and hidden partitions. Once created, the image is loaded into specialized software that investigators can use to review its contents without altering the original data. But even with these tools, we had no way to verify that what we were seeing was accurate or complete. We weren't the ones who made the image. We weren't even allowed to access the original laptop to compare. If something was left out—intentionally or not—we would never know.

Based on the strength of what little evidence we'd been able to get, Joe drafted search warrants that would have allowed agents to go in and see what else Hunter had in his home and office—a step that would have been done months ago if Hunter had been any other taxpayer. Joe also planned to interview about fifteen people, including business associates of Hunter's. The list also included family members who'd received direct payments from Hunter, accountants who'd prepared his taxes, and many others.

But now, with Joe Biden officially the Democratic Party's nominee for president, the real stonewalling began. Emails from the Department of Justice went unanswered. We didn't hear a thing about the list of witnesses we planned to interview.

Of course, something else had changed in the case, and it was a pretty big deal.

Hunter Biden had finally filed his taxes.

He hadn't exactly done it out of the goodness of his heart.

By mid-2019, Hunter Biden was juggling two lawsuits that placed an uncomfortable spotlight on his finances. The first was brought by his ex-wife, Kathleen Buhle, who had taken him to court in Washington, D.C., after he stopped making spousal support payments. Their separation agreement required him to provide financial records—including his tax returns—to determine how much he owed. But Hunter refused to turn over the documents, stalling for months and leaving Buhle's legal team scrambling to piece together his income.

Meanwhile in Arkansas, Lunden Roberts—the mother of his out-of-wedlock child—was fighting a similar battle. She had sued for child support after Hunter disappeared from their daughter's life, forcing the court to determine what he owed based on his earnings. But as in D.C., Hunter dragged his feet, declining to provide the financial disclosures necessary to calculate payments.

As both cases moved forward, patience ran thin. By the end of 2019, the courts had had enough. Judges in both D.C. and Arkansas ordered Hunter to hand over his 2017 and 2018 tax returns, setting back-to-back deadlines in mid-January 2020. He blew past both. That led to an ultimatum: produce the records or risk a contempt ruling that could land him in jail. With the threat of incarceration looming (as well as the possibility that he might eventually be called to testify in front of the Senate), Hunter finally got together with his accountants and began pulling together tax returns for him to submit.

The accountants, while sitting with Hunter at a table and going through his bank statements, became aware that he was attempting to classify numerous personal expenses—such as payments to prostitutes, luxury hotel stays, and even membership fees for a sex club—as business deductions. They flagged items, but Hunter insisted they were legitimate expenses. As a result, the accountants created a representation letter as a way to protect themselves, effectively putting the responsibility for any false claims directly on him. The letter stated that all reported income was accurate and all deductions were legitimate business expenses.

Even for good accountants, preparing taxes for Hunter Biden was a difficult task. Over the years, the man had constructed many legal entities to conceal and move around his money. They included, but were not limited to, Lion Hall Group LLC, Owasco P.C., Robinson Walker LLC, Skaneateles LLC, Seneca Global Advisers LLC, Rosemont Seneca Partners LLC, Rosemont Seneca Principal Investments LLC, Rosemont Realty LLC, Rosemont Seneca Thornton LLC, Rosemont Seneca Advisors LLC, Rosemont Seneca Bohai LLC, RSTP II Alpha Partners LLC, RSTP II Bravo Partners LLC, Owasco LLC, and Hudson West III LLC.

The money that flowed into these entities came from many different sources. Between 2016 and 2020, Hunter Biden had been paid millions of dollars by a web of foreign and domestic companies, each funneling cash into different LLCs and bank accounts under his control. These payments came from Ukrainian, Chinese, and Romanian business interests, as well as personal associates who helped sustain his lifestyle.

During his time on the board of Burisma Holdings, Hunter was paid approximately $1 million per year. His compensation was reduced in 2017 to about $500,000 annually, but by then he had already raked in over $1 million in 2016, $630,556 in 2017, $491,939 in 2018, and $160,207 in 2019. This money was wired in monthly installments often landing in accounts associated with his various business entities. In addition to Burisma, Hunter entered into a lucrative arrangement with a Romanian businessman referred to as "G.P." in 2015. Under an oral agreement, he was supposedly providing consulting services to help G.P. contest bribery charges in Romania. Payments were structured through a Romanian business associated with G.P., and between November 2015 and May 2017 G.P.'s entity sent approximately $3.1 million.

These funds were split roughly into thirds—one share for Hunter, and the rest divided among his business partners.

Then there were Hunter's dealings with CEFC China Energy Co., a Chinese conglomerate that sought to establish influence in U.S. business and political circles. Beginning in late 2015, Hunter and his business associates pursued infrastructure projects tied to CEFC. In December 2015, Hunter met with CEFC representatives in Washington, D.C. Over the next two years, he and his associates continued discussions, eventually meeting with CEFC's then chairman in February 2017.

That meeting bore fruit. On March 1, 2017, a Hong Kong–based CEFC affiliate wired $3 million to one of Hunter's business partner's entities, supposedly for deal sourcing and identifying business ventures. Hunter had an oral agreement to receive one-third of those funds, or about $1 million, some of which he redirected to another associate. Following that payment, Hunter and his team negotiated a joint venture with CEFC, which they called SinoHawk, but by the summer of 2017, Hunter went rogue. He cut out his former partners and instead negotiated a separate venture with CEFC known as Hudson West III (HWIII), securing even more lucrative payouts.

On August 2, 2017, Hunter signed an agreement on behalf of Owasco P.C., one of his primary business entities, to manage HWIII. The deal came with a $5 million capital contribution from another Chinese company, and Hunter was set to receive $100,000 per month, plus a one-time retainer of $500,000. That arrangement resulted in seven wire transfers to Owasco in 2017 totaling $1.445 million. These payments continued into 2018, with another fifteen transfers amounting to $2.1 million. From there, Hunter wired approximately $843,999 to another associate, distributing the money among his network.

Beyond these major deals, Hunter leveraged additional entities for payouts. His company Skaneateles LLC received $666,572 in September 2017, while another venture called Global, a firm with ties to trial attorneys in China and India, sent him a $619,000 distribution in March 2019.

As his business income fluctuated, Hunter also relied on direct financial support from personal acquaintances. Between January 2019 and October 2020, an entertainment lawyer—referred to as "Personal Friend"—provided him with over $1.2 million in financial assistance. This included payments to rent a lavish house on a canal in Venice, California ($200,000), make Porsche payments ($11,000), and cover other personal expenses.

By 2019, Hunter was also working on his memoir, *Beautiful Things*, in which he chronicled his addiction and personal struggles. The first installment of his book advance provided him with $140,625, which was deposited into his wife's bank account.

The accountants in California did the best they could to corral all this income and keep track of Hunter's deductions. And since Hunter had signed a representation letter that put the onus for all the information on himself—something Joe had never seen in all his years investigating tax criminals—the accountants were able to send them in without any danger that they might be punished or reprimanded.

Clearly, this wasn't the kind of thing innocent taxpayers were forced to do by their accountants.

Back at the IRS, we had our own problem. Once Hunter and his accountants finally filed his delinquent tax returns in February 2020, we needed to look at them. If they were anything like the ones Joe had seen during the early days of the investigation, they were sure to include more evidence of potential crimes. You might think this would be as simple as logging on to a computer database, typing in Hunter's name, and pulling up the returns in PDF format. You might think you could email someone at the IRS and have them show up in your inbox—or at least on your desk—the very next day. Sometimes, it does work like that. These days, when we need something it's usually just a few clicks or a phone call away.

During the early months of the pandemic, things were different. The people who usually opened the mail at the IRS stayed home along with everyone else. The same went for the people who answered the phones at taxpayer assistance centers, or TACs. This means that giant stacks of mail built up. Tax returns, letters of dispute, and other paper correspondence languished on desks. Then those stacks became piles, and the piles became unmanageable mountains. A few months into the stay-at-home orders, the IRS had semitrailers full of mail to dig through. Somewhere in one of them, among hundreds of thousands of pieces of taxpayer correspondence, were the copies of Hunter Biden's returns that we needed.

You might wonder why we weren't able to do any of this on the computer. The answer has to do with a strange quirk of the way the IRS processes late returns. When most people file their taxes, they do it online. But that's only an option when you're filing for the past year. When you wait three or four years to file, the way Hunter Biden did, you need to mail your returns to a processing center. Once a paper return arrives, it isn't immediately scanned into the system. Instead, an IRS employee physically stamps it with a "received" mark recording the date it was filed. After that, the return is assigned a unique document locator number (DLN), which allows the IRS to track it throughout processing. But even then, it doesn't go straight into the system. The return is routed through multiple steps—sometimes sitting in a queue—before it's eventually scanned, digitized, and entered into the IRS's database. These extra steps introduce delays that wouldn't exist with an e-filed return where information is instantly uploaded and processed. The IRS's reliance on these manual procedures is partly due to the limitations of its individual master file (IMF), a decades-old system that still governs how tax data is processed. And that's *before* everything shut down for about six months due to Covid.

So we knew that Hunter had filed his returns. We knew they were somewhere in a processing facility in California. We just didn't know where in that facility they were, or how to find them.

So we sent an agent, who ended up spending three grueling days in 2020 with a mask on his face and hundreds of envelopes in his arms, digging through them all to find the one that had come in from Hunter Biden. Every few minutes, he'd throw a pile of mail aside and walk back to a cubicle where a nice lady would hand him yet another pile. Then he'd sit at a foldout table at least twenty feet from the nearest human being and start rifling through envelopes, straining to read the fine print and locate the names of Hunter Biden's tax preparers. At the end of the first day, he called Gary with an update and said progress had been slow. At the end of the second, he sounded like he wanted to climb to the roof of the processing center and jump off. (Thankfully, the building is only two stories high, so we could have patched him up and gotten him right back to sifting through envelopes in no time.)

Near the middle of the guy's third day on the job, we were seriously beginning to wonder whether we were even looking in the right location. We wondered if Hunter had indeed filed his taxes at all, or if this was some kind of trick he'd pulled to delay having to reveal anything about his finances in court.

After months of searching, the returns were finally found. After being notified they were found, we were looking at PDF copies of the returns, trying to understand the various deductions and income streams Hunter had attempted to claim and checking them against what we knew about his finances. Again, this was complex work. But it was a blast compared to what we'd been doing over the past few days, which was waiting (and waiting, and doing some more waiting).

It took some time to finalize a clear report on what we knew about Hunter's finances. Clearly, most of the deductions were nonsense, and you didn't have to be a forensic accountant to see it. For one thing, he'd claimed about $389,000 in business travel on his 2018 returns. A cursory glance at his messages and emails for that year revealed that he hadn't done much traveling for business. What he *had* done, according to the records we'd seen, was bounce around expensive hotels and rented homes in the United States smoking crack and partying. During a tense meeting with the accountants who prepared his taxes, Hunter had circled payments for hotels, car rentals, and prostitutes as business expenses, attempting to reduce his taxable income. He'd done the same with payments to Lunden Roberts, whom he had on his payroll despite the fact that she didn't work for him. There were so many false deductions, in fact, that it was hard to know where to begin.

But we got working, trying to figure out what numbers were legitimate expenses and which ones were false. If nothing else, it was good to be working on something concrete again, pushing ahead without being told we had to stop by management. In the end, we came up with a list of false deductions and improper payments that was long enough to fill a full chapter of this book.

Every time Joe got information, he shared it with DOJ. We knew that sending around all the material we had on a given investigation was the only way to ensure we were working efficiently. It was, as a matter of fact, the reason we put so many different people from so many different agencies on a case to begin with. We assumed that everyone at the FBI and DOJ was doing the same with us.

But they weren't.

In late May, an FBI agent in Pittsburgh reviewing files came upon another document that mentioned Hunter Biden by name. Months earlier, Attorney General Bill Barr had designated Pittsburgh (or, more accurately, the U.S. Attorney's Office for the Western District of Pennsylvania) to serve as the intake office for all evidence relating to Ukraine. This particular document was an FBI report from 2017 that contained information from a "confidential human source," or CHS. The document, called an FD-1023, contained an explosive claim: Burisma had allegedly made a concerted effort to bribe Joe Biden with a $5 million payment.

On the surface, the source seemed credible. He had worked with the FBI for years providing information on cases unrelated to Burisma or the Bidens. If true, his story could have been one of the biggest political scandals in modern history.

But there was just one problem: the FBI had never been able to verify it.

As soon as the agent saw what was in the report, he pushed to reinterview the source hoping to corroborate key details. He wanted to go deeper on some of the allegations, just like we did. But at FBI headquarters, there was resistance. By this point, Joe Biden had officially secured enough delegates to clinch the Democratic nomination, and some in the bureau worried about the political implications of reviving an unverified claim. The fight dragged on for a month.

Finally, in late June 2020, the special agent interviewed the source again hoping to substantiate what had been in the original FD-1023. What he got was far more than he expected.

During the interview, the source laid out in explicit terms how everyone at Burisma understood the alleged bribery scheme. There was no ambiguity. Hunter Biden had been hired not for his expertise—because he had none in the oil and gas sector—but to serve as a shield, a layer of protection against legal scrutiny. Burisma's executives knew exactly what they were paying for. As one of them had previously stated, they had brought Hunter Biden onto the board to "protect us, through his dad, from all kinds of problems." Now, in this second interview, the source confirmed that protection came at a cost.

After the interview, the source provided a great deal of supplemental information, including details about direct payments allegedly made to Joe and Hunter Biden, records of suspicious wire transfers, and—perhaps most shocking—his claim that he had kept seventeen recordings as insurance. These recordings, he said, documented Burisma's dealings with the Bidens, including two tapes featuring Joe Biden himself and fifteen featuring Hunter. Additionally, the source turned over two documents that appeared to be financial records or wire transfers, which he said showed proof of payments made to the Bidens.

In a new FD-1023 written on June 29, 2020, the special agent recorded some of the most salient details from the second interview—things anyone looking into Hunter Biden's business dealings would want to know. Among other things, it contained details we hadn't yet uncovered about how Hunter began working for Burisma and what the executives at the company expected of him. Most surprisingly, it included the source's apparent claim that he had been forced to make the payments to the Bidens to get Ukrainian prosecutor general Viktor Shokin fired.

"It costs [a million] to pay one Biden, and 5 [million] to another Biden," the report read.

The source elaborated further, saying that he had been "pushed to pay" the Bidens and that he had been coerced into making the payments. The term he used in Russian, *poluchili*, could be translated as "got it" or "received it," but it was also common slang for being forced or extorted to pay.

"I hope you have some back-up [proof] for your words," the agent said to the source.

"I have many text messages and recordings that show I was coerced to make such payments," the source replied.

The most damning information, however, was his alleged response when asked whether investigators would ever be able to track down proof of these payments. The source laughed and said, "It will take them ten years to find the records."

For years, these allegations sat in government files, hidden from view. The FBI never shared it with us—the IRS agents actively investigating Hunter Biden on separate tax-related charges. If they had, then we could have helped corroborate or debunk key details. We could have traced the alleged payments, analyzed financial records, and determined whether the claims had any merit. But they never gave us the chance.

In the end, the confidential source—Alexander Smirnov—would admit to making false statements to the FBI. But he didn't plead guilty until August 2024—and only after Weiss's office indicted him not just for making false statements, but also on unrelated tax charges that significantly increased his legal jeopardy. To us, it looked like a cleanup operation. Weiss had come under fire for failing to investigate the allegations seriously and burying them. No one would ever have known about it but for a still-anonymous FBI whistleblower who provided the FBI FD-1023 form to Senator Chuck Grassley. We only learned of it when the senator released it publicly. Prosecuting Smirnov gave Weiss and the Biden administration a critical talking point to debunk the allegations. Meanwhile, the FBI had spent years shielding the 1023 report from scrutiny—even from investigators like us, who had access to Hunter's financial records and could have verified or dismissed the claims far earlier and much more thoroughly by actually gathering evidence on it's merits. But they knew that as soon as we saw the words "Joe Biden" on that form, we'd start asking questions they didn't want asked.

They also hid the 1023 from the public allowing rumors about it to spread. It bears mentioning, of course, that back in June 2020, the FBI didn't know that many of these allegations were not true. They believed they were. In fact, they corroborated many of the details themselves that month. There was, in other words, no excuse for them to hide the allegations about Joe and Hunter Biden from us. The only reason someone would do it is because they were afraid some other, more damaging information about Joe and Hunter would be revealed by anyone trying to substantiate the allegations.

But we didn't know what we didn't know.

All we *did* know was that something still felt very wrong about the case. And the anxiety of the people in charge grew with every step Joe Biden took toward the White House. We knew they were keeping things from us. We just didn't know what.

So we brought it up the chain.

On June 16, we met with James Robnett, the director of IRS field operations, to discuss our concerns about stonewalling. We told him that DOJ Tax had made a concerted effort to drag their feet concerning the search warrants and interviews of key witnesses, producing emails and meeting notes to corroborate our account.

By this point, we'd been told we needed to have "all our ducks in a row" before going overt. We were told that because we were dealing with a big political family, different standards applied. Any other taxpayer would have been charged with a crime years ago. But Hunter Biden had been allowed to carry on with his life because of who his father was. And because of bureaucratic incompetence at the IRS—including our issues with sorting through mail—it didn't look like he was going to be brought to justice anytime soon.

We were told to wait (again) while leadership discussed the issue.

While we waited, a draft of a search warrant came in from a special agent at the FBI—who had received Hunter Biden's laptop—for Blue Star Strategies, one of the companies Hunter was a paid consultant for and deeply involved with in connection to his work for Burisma. Among other things, the warrant contained information about "Political Figure 1," clearly a reference to Joe Biden.

There were good reasons for this.

Emails and communications recovered from the laptop showed that Hunter's relationship with Blue Star Strategies was closely tied to his position on the board of Burisma and that the firm had been hired, at least in part, to influence U.S. government officials on Burisma's behalf. In one now-public email, a Burisma executive even thanked Hunter for arranging a meeting with his father. These connections raised red flags about potential violations of the Foreign Agents Registration Act (FARA), and any comprehensive warrant would naturally include references to individuals who may have been involved, even tangentially.

In the email with the warrant attached—which was sent to Lesley Wolf, Joe, and two agents at the FBI—the FBI special agent noted how hard the team had worked on making sure the warrant was perfect. He wrote that he and the two FBI agents who had contributed to it had "talked enough for one week during a single day" that day.

For two days, we heard nothing.

Finally, Lesley Wolf wrote back.

"As a priority," she wrote, "someone needs to redraft attachment B. I am not sure what this is cut and pasted from but other than the attribution, location and identity stuff at the end, none of it is appropriate and within the scope of this warrant. Please focus on FARA evidence only. There should be nothing about Political Figure 1 in here."

Although we raised a few objections, we made the edits. And the message was clear. Although we were investigating Joe Biden's son—who, it seemed, had often involved his father in his shady overseas business dealings—none of our materials were supposed to mention Joe Biden. Even when we needed material that might be in one of Joe Biden's homes or storage units, we couldn't mention him. The document might leak to the press, and that would make the Biden campaign look bad. And in the summer of 2020, there was nothing that the leadership of the FBI wanted less than to make Joe Biden look bad. Doing so might help elect Donald Trump for a second time.

By this point, President Trump had openly declared war on the intelligence agencies, especially the FBI. He had been enraged during his first four years in office by the multiple investigations into his supposed ties to Russia—which, in the end, turned out to be based on lies and unsubstantiated rumors from shady sources. When it came to *these* lies, however, the FBI was never shy about sharing details with anyone who wanted to see them. That included the press. For years, while the Russia collusion investigation was still going on, we read front-page stories about it, all sourced to "people with knowledge of the matter."

Consider the infamous Steele dossier. This was a long document compiled by a former British spy named Christopher Steele. It contained allegations that were a thousand times more ridiculous than anything in the FD-1023 the FBI had about Joe Biden. Among other things, it alleged that Donald Trump had been an agent of the Russian government since the 1980s and that Vladimir Putin had footage of him forcing prostitutes to urinate on his hotel bed. Rather than keeping this secret in the interest of "optics," the FBI leaked it to the press, which reported on it for months on end. The phrase "pee tape" entered the cultural lexicon. From then on, every time there was a new development in the Crossfire Hurricane case, some reporter at *The New York Times* heard about it.

There were serious differences in investigative methods as well. For instance, the FBI used the Steele dossier to obtain FISA warrants to surveil members of the Trump campaign. They also altered evidence in order to renew those warrants and omitted evidence that would have contradicted their findings. For nearly four years, the FBI went at Donald Trump—who, when the investigation started, was a leading candidate for president just like Joe Biden would be four years later—with everything it had. They were never shy about taking big swings on the investigation in public, and they didn't care at all about the optics of what they were doing.

So when it was implied that simply having Joe Biden's name on a warrant would be bad optics because it might leak to the press, it was hard to believe this represented some kind of long-standing policy at the Justice Department or the FBI. Traditionally, these agencies would stand down an investigation sixty or ninety days out from an election. We were outside that territory. And perhaps more importantly, Hunter Biden wasn't *running* in any election. But as the weeks turned into months, it became increasingly clear that our superiors had one goal in mind. They wanted to drag their feet on the investigation long enough to get us within that ninety-day window. That way, they could delay the investigation—or close it down entirely—on the pretense that continuing it might affect the outcome of the presidential election.

Again, this had never bothered them before. But now that Joe Biden was the nominee, everyone seemed terribly concerned about it. This was especially true given that Biden was running against a president who had promised several times over to do a complete overhaul of our intelligence agencies, stripping security clearances and rooting out political bias. It should go without saying that no one we were working with at the time would have done very well during an audit of political bias.

Still, we kept digging. We figured that if we got enough good evidence, delaying the case further would be impossible. We had emails, text messages, and financial records proving that Hunter had failed to pay his taxes and that he'd engaged in the kind of financial behavior that would have landed most people in jail a long time ago. I'm sure that by this point in the book, you're already tired of hearing us say that. But back then, Joe needed to repeat it to himself often. As the investigation kept getting sidetracked and slow-walked, it was important to keep telling himself the truth to remind himself he hadn't gone crazy. *This investigation is worthwhile,* he'd say, *and so is the pursuit of justice. If we make exceptions for this guy, it'll set a dangerous precedent. Keep working. Do your job.*

In late August, we got the kind of evidence we'd been waiting for. The results of a search warrant for Hunter Biden's iCloud account had finally come in, and they were stranger than we ever could have imagined. There were more photos than we'd seen before. More messages, too. The picture we'd been filling in for months just got a whole lot bigger. Because of evidence we'd seen raising the question of Joe Biden's involvement, as we combed through the evidence, searching the files using our proprietary software, we wondered if we might come across anything that might directly implicate Joe Biden.

Which, in a long string of WhatsApp messages we'd never seen before, is exactly what we got.

It appeared that on July 30, 2017, Hunter Biden wrote a message to Zhao Jiaming, the head of CEFC. It read:

"Z - Please have the director call me – not James or Tony or Jim – have him call me tonight. I am sitting here with my father and we would like to understand why the commitment made has not been fulfilled. I am very concerned that the Chairman has either changed his mind and broken our deal without telling me or that he is unaware of the promises and assurances that have been made have not been kept. Tell the director that I would like to resolve this now before it gets out of hand. And now means tonight. And Z if I get a call or text from anyone involved in this other than you, Zhang or the Chairman I will make certain that between the man sitting next to me and every person he knows and my ability to forever hold a grudge that you will regret not following my direction. All too often people mistake kindness for weakness – and all too often I am standing over top of them saying I warned you. From this moment until whenever he reaches me. It [is] 9:45 AM here and I assume 9:45 PM there so his night is running out."

A few minutes later, Zhao responded, "Copy. I will call you on Whatsapp."

Hunter replied, "Ok my friend – I am sitting here waiting for the call with my father. I sure hope whatever it is you are doing is very very very important."

There was a little more. But the thrust of the messages was clear. Hunter specifically claimed his father was involved in his business negotiations. This flew directly in the face of Joe Biden's various claims that he had never discussed or conducted business with his son. If these messages were accurate, Joe Biden had done both things, literally making threats to get a deal done. There were serious tax implications to this conversation, given that the "commitments" that hadn't been fulfilled almost certainly involved money changing hands. If Joe or Hunter got money as a result of these conversations, we needed to know it.

In messages that were sent a few days later, Hunter outlined a plan with Zhao for a "10M per annum budget to use to further the interest of the JV. This move to 5M is completely new to me and is not acceptable obviously... I can make $5M in salary at any law firm in America. If you think this is about money it's not. The Biden's [sic] are the best I know at doing exactly what the Chairman wants from this partnership. Please let's not quibble over peanuts."

We noted that Hunter said the *Bidens*, with an "s" (and an apostrophe, apparently typed in error), not *I*. He could have meant him and his uncle James. It was also possible, we knew, that Hunter was lying about his father sitting right beside him. One way to narrow the possibilities was to determine what location the message was sent from. If it was sent from Joe Biden's residence, that would increase the likelihood, in our eyes, that Hunter had been telling the truth.

We brought this up in a meeting of the prosecution team. Joe sent around an agenda that showed "location data" as the second or third item.

We were rebuffed immediately and told that the attorneys would think about it.

When it came to anything involving Joe Biden, we always were.

FOUR

THE JUICE AND THE SQUEEZE

FROM THE MOMENT Joe dialed into the conference line on September 3, 2020, he knew the call wasn't going to go well for him.

For one thing, the prosecutors had been silent on most of his requests for a few days. Search warrants hadn't been coming back. His questions had gone unanswered. Now they were going to try to run through everything in a phone call, which was never a good sign. A few hours before the call, Joe had sent around an email with a list of things he wanted to discuss.

It read:

Morning Everyone—

Agenda for today's call:

1. Electronic Production
  1. Status of the 4 Apple iCloud Backups
    1. Location Information – Is this still important?
    2. Relevancy review of the iPhone Backup from Laptop
    3. Email search warrant of BlueStar email accounts
    4. Supplemental Email Search Warrant (Title 18)
    5. Electronic Search Warrant of DropBox
      1. Dropbox has been preserved

    2. Emails that are not in our dataset
    6. Vadym (Gmail and Burisma Email Accounts) and Archer (@Burisma) – Discuss 2703-D Order
    7. Overall Timeline Production – Still in Process
    8. Quality Control of Relativity / Filter Review
2. Misc. Items:
    1. Status of SDNY additional emails requested
    2. Status of ▮▮▮▮ / Comerica ▮▮▮▮
        1. Updates on this information
    3. Interview Prep / Prosecution team continuing to work through this – See attached word document
    4. Physical search warrant for the residence Draft
    5. Misc. Pittsburgh Case
    6. Misc. Senate Investigation

Talk to everyone in a few hours!!

Joseph A. Ziegler
Special Agent

Now, as he sat waiting for everyone to join, he prepared to run down these items. The most important things were the physical search warrants the team had drafted related to Hunter Biden. We'd seen several emails and messages that led us to believe there might be important paper records that were relevant to the investigation in Joe Biden's residence and his guest house, where Hunter had stayed for long stretches of time. We believed we had achieved enough probable cause to go in and search these places.

Everyone logged on. After a few introductions and pleasantries, Lesley Wolf ran down the list for Joe, letting the team know why they'd be able to do little to none of what they planned. Joe and the team would continue to wait on a decision regarding the location data for the WhatsApp messages they'd been going through for a few days now. They would not be able to do a search of the Biden residences because of "optics." When Joe said they had met the standard of probable cause, Wolf agreed. Yet she said that probable cause was not a question in determining if a physical search warrant was legally viable.

"There is more than enough probable cause," she said. "But that's not the question. The question is whether the juice is worth the squeeze."

As Joe understood it, the "juice" in this case was the evidence that was necessary to make their case—evidence that would have been collected long ago if they were dealing with any other taxpayer. The "squeeze" was a routine search of a home that the IRS had probable cause to believe contained evidence of crimes. Apparently, having the details of this investigation leak to the media was a risk the prosecution team was not willing to take.

Near the end of the call, Wolf turned everyone's attention to a few electronic search warrants and document requests that Joe had drawn up. Wolf didn't say much about the legality of these warrants or when they'd be approved. Yet she went so far as to direct that they remove the name "Hunter Biden" from them.

Joe was shocked.

We'd kind of understood (but not really) why you'd want to remove Joe Biden's name from anything involving this investigation. The man was running for president, and he'd only been involved in these potential crimes in an ancillary way. But removing the name of *the person who was being investigated* was unprecedented. Joe had never done anything like it before. He spoke up about it, practically yelling into his phone.

"We can't do that. It's . . . I mean, it's just unethical."

There was dead silence on the line.

Finally, Wolf suggested we move on. She let us know that the search warrants for Blue Star Strategies—the ones we'd earlier been forced to remove Joe Biden's name from—would probably not be approved. They were sitting on someone's desk, and people "way above us" did not want them to go through. So they probably wouldn't. This was a significant blow to the piece of the case that relied on violations of the Foreign Agents Registration Act.

The call didn't last much longer. Joe raised a few more objections. So did Gary. But they were ignored. Things were tense as everyone hung up the phones and went about their business. As Joe got back to his work, he kept thinking about the phrase Lesley Wolf had used regarding the now-aborted search of the Biden residences.

The question is whether the juice is worth the squeeze.

This, he realized, perfectly encapsulated the view of his superiors toward this case. No one doubted that Hunter Biden had probably committed crimes. Everyone seemed to know that if we were allowed to go forward as usual, the future president's son would probably end up indicted. They just didn't think pursuing justice as usual was worth the media uproar that would ensue. Again, this was not a concern when the intelligence community was investigating Donald Trump for his alleged (and false) ties to Russia. It wasn't a concern during investigations into Paul Manafort, Roger Stone, or Michael Flynn, either.

For the Bidens, the rules were different.

Joe was still repeating that phrase in his mind (*the juice isn't worth the squeeze, the juice isn't worth . . .*) the next morning when he got another email from Lesley Wolf. She wanted to "hop on the phone" at 9:45 to follow up on some of the things they'd discussed the previous day. Joe said he was around, and a few minutes later, he was on another phone call.

This time, the news came from individuals "way over our heads." One of them was Deputy Attorney General Richard

Donoghue. A seasoned attorney and prosecutor, Donoghue had previously served as the United States attorney for the Eastern District of New York before being appointed as the acting deputy attorney general in late 2020.

As Wolf conveyed during the call, Donoghue had issued a directive for all "politically sensitive cases" to refrain from overt activities until after the general election. This meant no search warrants or interviews; essentially, we were to stand down until further notice despite the fact that Hunter Biden was not a candidate for anything. At the end of the call, Wolf remarked, "Right now, the DOJ is under fire, and that is self-inflicted. We need to repair our reputation."

It wasn't entirely clear what she was referencing, but Joe suspected it related to recent controversies surrounding the Department of Justice, including allegations of political bias and the handling of high-profile investigations. These issues had placed the DOJ under intense public scrutiny, leading to internal efforts to restore its standing and impartiality.

Again, those efforts hardly seemed fair when they resulted in treating this presidential election different than earlier ones. But it didn't matter. Orders were orders. As much as we didn't like them—and as much as we had complained about them to the people directly over our heads—we hadn't yet reached a point where we were ready to blow the whistle or directly disobey. For the most part, we went about our lives and focused on other things, still doing the day-to-day work on the Hunter Biden case and waiting until we could finally go overt. Shortly after the call, we made plans to do just that on November 17, about two weeks after the election. We figured that would be more than enough time, even with the strange voting procedures that had been inaugurated for the pandemic.

By November 17, surely, we'd know whether the next president would be Joe Biden or Donald Trump. There was no reason to think there'd be any theatrics or drama concerning the outcome. If Trump won, our superiors would no longer have to be afraid that our investigation would impede Joe Biden's chances of becoming president. If Biden won, the same thing would happen. Once the "big guy" was safely in the White House, they could no longer claim that bringing his son to justice would affect the outcome of the election. After all, we didn't think they'd try to delay the case forever.

On this, and so many other things, we were very wrong.

By the fall of 2020, we had come up with a list of fifteen people we wanted to interview before the Sportsman case could be considered complete. It hadn't changed at all since Joe first drew it up. The most important interviews were with Hunter's accountants, his business partners, and his family members.

Each one of these people had information we needed. All of them had interacted with Hunter in some way, usually through cryptic messages that we believed required further explanation. We'd shown this list to our superiors many times, and we hadn't heard any pushback on anything.

Until September 21, when we had yet another call filled with bad news.

On this call, the FBI let us know that they only wanted us to do five of these interviews. Leadership at the bureau wanted to assess whether they should remain involved at all. Later that afternoon, Gary learned that one of the special agents assigned to the case had just moved back to Wilmington, Delaware, where he'd grown up. He had told others he was concerned about the consequences for him and his family if he conducted sensitive interviews around that town involving the Bidens. He definitely didn't want to pull up to the Biden guest house, which sat just a few miles from his own home, and start poking around.

It was exactly the kind of thing Joe had been afraid of during the struggle for venue. This was why he'd fought so hard to keep the case out of Delaware in the first place. He knew that eventually we'd end up working with someone who didn't want to tarnish his or her reputation among the Delaware legal community by going too hard at the Bidens. As Hunter had shown in his WhatsApp messages to CEFC's Zhao, he and the rest of the Biden family knew how to hold a grudge. Even a cursory glance through Hunter's emails and text messages revealed many threats for retribution. Sometimes, these threats were even made within the family.

The fear of that kind of retribution seemed to have already kept us from bringing a case against Hunter Biden. Even though we had all the probable cause we needed, we hadn't been allowed to move forward due to political concerns. As it happened, though, we weren't the only ones looking. On September 23, for instance, Senator Chuck Grassley released a report on an investigation he was conducting with Senator Ron Johnson into the Biden family. Joe read it as soon as it came out, grinding his teeth at how shallow the inquiry was. All around him was evidence that the public deserved to know about, especially before an election. And the Senate offices investigating didn't have access to it.

But the senators did find a great deal of information. They knew about the $3.5 million wire transfer Hunter Biden received from Elena Baturina, the wife of the former mayor of Moscow, a transaction that had never been adequately explained. They knew about the millions of dollars in questionable transactions Hunter and his associates had with Chinese nationals linked to the Communist Party and the People's Liberation Army, including Ye Jianming and Gongwen Dong. They even found that Hunter Biden had opened a joint bank account with Gongwen Dong, which financed a $100,000 global spending spree for James and Sara Biden.

The report also detailed Hunter's involvement in payments to Russian and Eastern European women—the same payments that had led Joe to start the investigation in the first place. Then there was the revelation that Hunter had moved millions of dollars from his law firm into James and Sara Biden's firm, a transaction that raised red flags at the bank. When investigators questioned it, Sara Biden refused to provide documentation leading the bank to close the account entirely.

Even beyond foreign money, the senators uncovered how Hunter Biden was serving on Burisma's board at the same time its owner, Mykola Zlochevsky, allegedly paid a $7 million bribe to Ukrainian officials to shut down an investigation into his company. State Department official George Kent had raised concerns about this as early as 2015, but they were ignored. Another senior official, Amos Hochstein, went so far as to warn Joe Biden personally that Hunter's Burisma ties were undermining U.S. policy and enabling Russian disinformation.

This wasn't speculation. It wasn't based on political rumors or opposition research. It was the result of real financial records, real government reports, and real national security concerns. And yet, despite everything the Senate offices uncovered, it still barely scratched the surface of what we knew.

And for now, we had to keep quiet about what we knew—at least until after the election was over.

Unfortunately, not everyone had the same directive.

Joe saw the *New York Post* headline for the first time on Twitter. It was late in the evening on October 14.

"Smoking-gun email reveals how Hunter Biden introduced Ukrainian businessman to VP dad," the headline read. Joe clicked through and saw a blown-up version of the next morning's print edition. It was a photo of Joe and Hunter Biden from years earlier beside giant white letters reading: "Biden Secret Emails" in bold white type. Above it, the tagline was *"Revealed: Ukrainian exec thanked Hunter Biden for 'opportunity to meet' veep dad."*

This was information we'd been sitting on for months.

From the first lines of the article, Joe could tell that the reporters at the *Post* hadn't had access to the laptop for very long. He wondered how they'd gotten it in the first place. It was hard not to feel slightly irritated. Since early 2020, he and his team had been working diligently to confirm that the messages on the laptop were valid. They'd formed a detailed database of messages that was cross-referenced to other materials they'd obtained from search warrants. They understood what was on the laptop better than almost anyone in the country—certainly better than Hunter himself, who'd been high on crack for most of the events these messages memorialized.

Joe knew there would be more stories. If the reporters—who, it was revealed in later reporting, were extremely hesitant to attach their bylines to the story in the first place given rumors that the laptop was Russian disinformation—had the kind of access to the laptop that Joe thought they did, news would break every hour between now and the election. But the story that everyone seemed the most interested in (certainly the news outlets that

Joe tended to follow) had nothing to do with what was on the laptop. They were about the provenance of the laptop itself. Serious outlets such as *The New York Times* and *Bloomberg* openly asserted that the laptop was fake and that the messages had been doctored by Russian hackers.

On the night the story was posted, executives at Twitter called the FBI. The story was being widely shared on Twitter at the time. It had been retweeted hundreds of thousands of times already. During the call, someone at Twitter asked the agents on the call—we, of course, were not among them—whether the material on the laptop was authentic. If their platform was allowing the spread of Russian misinformation, they wanted to know.

According to later testimony of someone who was on the call, at first only one agent spoke up. She began to say, "Yes, it is." But before she could get past "Y—," another agent cut her off.

"No further comment."

The implication was clear. And it was clear, in part, because some people at the FBI had been conditioning social media companies to believe that "hack-and-dump" operations were going to be commonplace during the 2020 election. For months, agents had warned that negative information about Joe Biden might come out, and that when it did, it was probably going to be Russian disinformation. One of these agents, Elvis Chan, later admitted to meeting weekly with major tech companies and warning them in advance that a Russian "hack-and-leak" campaign could target the Biden family specifically.

Combined with that, the FBI's refusal to say that the laptop was real gave Twitter very good reason to think they were dealing with Russian disinformation. Just a few hours after that first story was published, Twitter banned the *Post*'s story from being shared, even in private messages. It also locked the newspaper—which, as several sources have pointed out since, is the oldest one in the United States, founded by Alexander Hamilton himself—out of its Twitter account.

There were more stories, as we had known there would be. One of them, published just one day after the initial story, concerned the email from James Gilliar to Tony Bobulinski laying out the proposed equity split in a Chinese business venture. The phrase "ten percent for the big guy" soon began making its way around Twitter, even with the story censored. Given how easy it was to google the phrase and end up at the *Post*'s website anyway, the decision for Twitter to censor it in the first place was beginning to seem like a disastrous PR move. It certainly gave the impression that they were protecting the Biden family from true information—which they were.

Rumors swirled. Many people who read these stories wondered, and not without good reason, why the existence of the laptop had remained a secret for this long. The cloak-and-dagger nature of the stories—not to mention the fact that many high-level members of the government were now coming out and lying about the laptop—gave people a bad taste in their mouths. The most serious breach of public trust came on October 19, when fifty-one former members of the intelligence community signed a letter stating that the laptop had "all the classic earmarks of a Russian information operation."

Many of these officials had names that were familiar to the American people. They'd testified in front of Congress. They'd made statements on behalf of the government. Most if not all of them still had contacts in the FBI. They could have found out if the laptop was genuine or not. But instead, they wrote this strange document—which, oddly enough, cited media reports about Rudy Giuliani rather than the kind of hard evidence that intel agents are supposed to deal with—and published it on the internet. Hours later, *Politico* posted the headline: "Hunter Biden story is Russian disinfo, dozens of former intelligence officials say." Reading the story, anyone would have believed them. If Joe hadn't been working this case for the past few years, *he* would have believed them.

Most of his friends did. Like these intelligence officials, they didn't want Donald Trump to win the election. They had talked themselves into being excited about Joe Biden just like millions of other Democrats around the country. By the time we were a few weeks out from the election, discussion of Russian interference was common. Joe never discussed the details of his work with his family, let alone their friends. But it was hard not to blurt out everything he knew when news like the intel letter was floating around. For the first time in his life, he had proof that everyone—top intelligence officials, news organizations, and political candidates—was lying. And almost all of them *knew* they were lying. It was a bewildering feeling.

The only solace was that they'd go overt soon. Early that October, Lesley Wolf had emailed Joe to let him know that David Weiss, the United States attorney who'd been overseeing the investigation, had approved the day of action. On November 17, we'd send agents out to cities all over the country to carry out interviews and serve document requests. That same day, Gary had emailed George Murphy, his IRS assistant special agent in charge, saying, "There has been some discussion that the USAO is uncomfortable with conducting the subject interview of Sportsman while he is in Delaware (this is a possibility if conducted closer to Thanksgiving on 11/26)." He still hadn't heard back. Either way, though, it seemed that we would be going overt soon.

We didn't have much choice. Given how many news stories there were about Hunter and his shady business dealings, it was only a matter of time before someone—possibly a journalist who didn't know all the facts—began piecing together our investigation in public. If our superiors thought we'd have had problems going overt weeks ago, they had no idea how bad things could get when stories began appearing on the cover of the *New York Post* about all the implications that the laptop's contents might have on Hunter's taxes. At the very least, it would make us look incompetent. At worst, it would make us look corrupt for not finishing the investigation sooner.

On October 19, shortly after the letter about "Russian disinfo" was published online, Gary emailed Lesley Wolf.

"We need to talk about the computer," he wrote. "It appears the FBI is making certain representations about the device and the only reason we know what is on that device is because of the IRS-CI affiant search warrant that allowed access to the contents. If Durham also executed on [sic] search warrant on the device we need to know so that my leadership is informed. My management has to be looped into whatever the FBI is doing with the laptop. It is IRS-CI's responsibility to know what is happening. Also, if the FBI is planning to release information to anybody we need to be looped in as it [is] possible that data could have various disclosure requirements unique to the IRS. Let me know when I can be briefed on this issue."

Shortly thereafter, Wolf emailed back and set up a meeting between the prosecution team and the computer analysts at the FBI who had combed through the laptop's contents and created the digital image we'd been using to search it. Finally, we were going to get answers on who knew what about the laptop, when they knew it, and what else might be out there. For the next few days, we prepared questions for the meeting, looking forward to working productively with the FBI after so many weeks of stonewalling.

One phone call from around this time stands out in Gary's memory. He was driving in a car with one of his agents. He called the special agent in charge at the time. For a few seconds, he attempted to give her updates that she could pass up to the chief of the IRS Criminal Investigation Division. She said the chief did not want to know any details. When Gary attempted to tell *her* the details he wanted to pass up, she cut him off.

"Gary," she said. "I do not want to know anything I don't need to know."

This seemed to sum up everyone's thoughts on the Hunter Biden investigation.

And it went both ways, as we were about to find out.

The tech guys spoke quickly—so quickly, in fact, that Gary's hand cramped as he tried to take notes on what they were saying.

For a few hours, the team reviewed everything they'd done from the moment they learned Hunter's laptop existed until the present. By the end of the meeting, Gary had a timeline of every step that had occurred throughout the process. One of the most interesting items came on March 31, 2020, when the team said that "for a variety of reasons," they had decided to withhold the contents of the laptop from the prosecution team. This was a policy they had largely stuck to throughout the course of the investigation, only allowing us access to small amounts of data.

Joe interrupted at one point and asked, "Shouldn't we see everything? If we're going to have to testify to this material later, shouldn't we see it?"

"We can talk about that later," said Lesley Wolf. "This is a historical review."

This didn't make much sense to Gary.

The meeting was almost over when Wolf addressed the possibility that things might have been added to the computer. Third parties had alleged this—many of them working in the media. While we'd crosschecked many of the emails sent from the laptop with records from other sources, that wouldn't tell us whether some fake content was dumped on the hard drive after it had left Hunter Biden's possession. But the FBI had technical means of assessing this, such as examining CSV (or "change sequence value") lists, which give the ability to tell when things were added to a computer. And Wolf said that after careful review, we had no reason to believe that anyone had added anything to the laptop. The contents were legitimate.

Yet the American people still didn't know that. At the very moment we were sitting together talking about the history of the laptop within the FBI, "misinformation" was spreading about it in the media. Oddly enough, the "misinformation" said that the contents of the laptop (which were verifiably true) were themselves a Russian disinformation campaign. We'd held back all this information from the public under the guise of trying *not* to interfere with an election. And now, with just weeks to go before voters headed to the polls, it seemed that we were doing just that. It was becoming increasingly clear to us that what the IRS, FBI, and DOJ were worried about wasn't interfering in the election; it was interfering in a way that might help Donald Trump or hurt Joe Biden. They were perfectly fine with lying by omission—which, no matter how you slice it, is *exactly* what we did by withholding information about the veracity of the laptop. They just didn't want to give the Trump campaign any ammunition it could use to further denigrate American intelligence agencies or claim the election was being swayed on behalf of the Democrats.

But that's what was happening.

A few days before the meeting, DOJ Tax had denied our request to do a "walk-by" of Hunter Biden's residence. In law enforcement, a "walk-by" is brief, informal surveillance of a location, typically conducted from a public vantage point to gather preliminary intelligence without alerting the subject. It's often used to assess the surroundings, identify potential security concerns, confirm a subject's presence, or establish patterns of movement before executing a more formal operation. We planned to do one so we could be fully prepared for our interview of Hunter in mid- to late November. Once again, if this had been any other investigation, we would have done it years ago. But those at the DOJ denied it, and they didn't give a reason. Then they denied our search warrant for the residence, even as they acknowledged we had met probable cause. Again, no reason was given.

Something similar occurred surrounding an October 23 meeting with the U.S. Attorney's Office for the Western District of Pennsylvania. Prosecutors there had been asking for weeks to meet with the District of Delaware prosecutors on the Hunter Biden case in order to pass along information from their review of Ukraine-related allegations. Today, we know that included the now-infamous FBI FD-1023 with the Biden bribery allegations, but neither we nor Lesley Wolf knew that at the time. Still, Wolf made clear to our investigative team she didn't want to take the meeting. She erroneously believed all their information was from Rudy Giuliani and skeptically derided it as conspiracy fodder. We felt we needed to know the Hunter Biden information because there might be tax implications. Yet when we requested to attend the briefing with the rest of the prosecution team, we were denied. No one told us why. And after the meeting, Wolf certainly didn't share with us the damning allegations provided to her, like the two-month-old FD-1023.

By this point, Gary had begun carefully documenting everything that was said in meetings or on phone calls regarding the case. It was becoming clear to him that someday soon, when the investigation was over, he'd need to speak with someone about all the wrong moves that had been made. So he memorialized everything. He did this, by the way, against the advice of his superiors, who often told him not to put any communications in writing when he could help it. Their view seemed to be "the less we email, the less we'll have to answer for later." Given all he'd seen, Gary took the opposite view. He believed that if he wasn't doing anything wrong, there was no reason not to document all of it. And when he saw delays, he made sure to document them—which, by this point, was keeping him very busy.

The pattern was becoming so familiar that it was almost comical. One day we'd be told about groundbreaking information that the entire prosecution team needed to see. Then, when we asked to see it, we'd be told it wasn't important. To this day, we're not sure whether we got this treatment because we weren't perceived to be as friendly to the Bidens (and to Democrats in general) as everyone else working the case. If that's what our leadership thought, it wasn't true. At the time, Joe was firmly a Democrat. Gary was mostly apolitical. But that didn't matter when it came to internal politics. We had gone too hard at Hunter Biden, and our superiors believed we couldn't be trusted.

Around this time, the Hunter Biden investigation split in two. The one we were running was conducted by the book. We sought to charge ahead in a timely manner just like we'd been taught. But we didn't have all the information. The other investigation was conducted by people who had all the information but didn't want to do anything with it—who, in fact, *hid* the information from anyone who might do something with it. This was deeply troubling for a few reasons. One was that when the public, or the United States Congress, did a review of this investigation when it was over, they wouldn't see it as two separate investigations; they would see it all as one. The mistakes of our superiors would be seen as our mistakes if we didn't do something to prevent that from happening. Documenting the steps of the investigation was one thing we could do to prevent that, and Gary recorded details whenever he could.

The other step was to blow the whistle.

Technically, this is an option available to all government employees who see corruption at their places of work. There are protections in place, most of which fall under the Whistleblower Protection Act, a federal law designed to shield employees from retaliation when they report misconduct, abuse of authority, or violations of law within the government. Joe had heard the term used before, most often in connection with the case of Edward Snowden, but he hadn't yet thought about it in connection with our case. Gary hadn't either. In truth, neither of us had a real understanding of what "blowing the whistle" meant. We only knew that it was a last-ditch option for people who'd seen things at their workplace that they could no longer tolerate. We knew there were protections, but we didn't know how strong they were.

It wasn't something we were ready to do.

Not yet, at least.

FIVE

DAY OF INACTION

ON ELECTION NIGHT 2020, Joe stood in his living room surrounded by friends. He and David had decided to have a few people over and watch the returns come in. Even though they wouldn't know the winner that night (or, if you believed the news, for a few weeks), they figured it would be good to have people around.

Things had been rough, and not just because of the case.

Back in February 2019, Joe's father had been told he had between six and twelve months to live. Now, almost two years later, he was still hanging in there, living in Joe's hometown in Northeast Ohio. Joe hadn't been able to go back nearly as often as he wanted to because of travel restrictions imposed by the pandemic. This was devastating for a few reasons, chief among them that Joe and his father still had some unfinished emotional business to deal with. As a kid, Joe had often felt like a disappointment to his dad, who was a retired machinist and the kind of man who believed emotions were something to be suppressed, not expressed. One of the things Robert Ziegler often said to his son before he left the house was, "Do not come home with a boyfriend, Joe." The shame of being gay got so bad that Joe did end up marrying a woman at the age of twenty-nine, trying to do what his dad expected of him. He divorced his wife after only ten months when it became clear they wouldn't be able to have children together. Since then, Joe's relationship with his father had been tense. Robert knew Joe was in a relationship with a man and that he seemed happy. But they didn't talk about it often. On the infrequent occasions that Joe went home to spend time with his father, they tended to speak about sports and the weather. The elephant in the room rarely came up.

On top of all that, David's mother had been diagnosed with breast cancer. She'd moved in with Joe and David so she could recover from a double mastectomy. David had stayed home with her for long hours, taking so many days off work as a personal trainer that his job was in jeopardy. Joe was happy that he and David could help, but the emotional pressure was beginning to build. By election night, he was worried about David's job as well as his own. Eventually, he feared things might get so tense between him and IRS management that he might be fired from his job, leaving his growing family without any income. There were times when he wondered whether he should just back off his controversial case and keep his superiors happy.

But those thoughts never lasted for very long. If nothing else, Joe did his job by the book. He wasn't going to take it easy on anyone or stop doing the steps that were required of him just because it might ruffle some feathers at his agency. That would remain true whether Donald Trump or Joe Biden ended up in the White House.

Which, as of about ten o'clock at night on November 3, 2020, was uncertain. Throughout the evening, returns had looked good for President Trump. This had caused some consternation among the folks gathered in Joe's living room, nearly all of whom were supporting Biden. To them, as well as millions of good liberals all over the country, Biden was seen as a unifier—a stabilizing force who would return the country to peace and harmony after four years of what they saw as unmediated chaos. Every time someone spouted this talking point, of course, Joe couldn't help but think of the chaos that had gone on with the Biden family behind the scenes. Hunter Biden, who'd attempted (quite possibly with success, as far as we knew at the time) to bring his dad in on corrupt business deals overseas, had written many messages about the dysfunction surrounding his father.

Those messages were far from Joe's mind when he went to sleep on election night. He assumed, like many other Americans, that things would swing in President Trump's favor. The next morning, when it became clear that this wasn't going to happen, thoughts of work hit him once again. He wondered what this meant for the case. If Joe Biden became president, it was possible that leadership at the FBI, the DOJ, and the IRS might allow the investigation to continue unimpeded. If their goal really was to get Joe Biden into the White House, they would have achieved that. But Joe got the sense that they wouldn't stop now that Biden was in office, if only because moving forward with the investigation might cause the public to wonder what took so long. He began to feel that their strategy was not simply to delay the investigation, but to kill it altogether—doing so slowly by pushing things back so far that the statute of limitations ran out on the evidence.

This concern crystalized on November 10, when David Weiss organized a conference call with the prosecution team. For the most part, we hadn't interacted with Weiss in a direct way throughout the case. His orders had come in through his subordinates, such as Lesley Wolf. On this call, though, he spoke for himself, telling the team that the planned day of action on November 17 could not go forward as planned. As long as President Trump was contesting the results of the election, the Department of Justice was going to stay quiet about any investigations into the Biden family.

And that was that.

At least for now.

In the following weeks, pressure mounted to investigate Joe Biden in a public way. People had begun to feel that things were being kept from them. We knew the feeling. On November 17, the *New York Post*, which had finally gotten its Twitter account reinstated, published an editorial calling for David Weiss to be named special counsel. It was, the paper insisted, the only way to ensure accountability and independence.

"Okay," Gary said. "We're now turning to page four."

He'd been sitting in a conference room at the offices of the Delaware U.S. attorney for about four hours planning for the team's upcoming "day of action." About twelve other people sat around the table with him, including Lesley Wolf. It was December 3, 2020. After a great deal of wrangling, leadership had agreed to a new day of action on December 8. If all went according to plan, we were set to go overt that morning. Our agents would finally get the chance to interview Hunter Biden as well as fourteen people tied to the case.

But first, we needed to rehearse. Unlike what you might think from watching the movies, federal agents don't just turn up at people's doors and start asking whatever questions come to mind. They go into their interviews with a plan. Usually, this plan takes the form of a detailed outline. The more complicated the case, the more detailed the outline. In the case of Rob Walker, a longtime business associate of Hunter Biden, the outline was about fourteen pages long. And the font was small. It contained questions that the special agents wanted to ask about everything from Hunter's relationship with Walker to the various emails they'd sent back and forth about business. The plan was to start small, developing a rapport with Walker, and then ask the questions we really wanted answers to. The most pressing question, Gary knew, came in the middle of page four. That morning, the agent read that question aloud, articulating it just as he planned to on our day of action.

"We have an email here," he said. "And ... I guess, here, I'll quote from the email and show him. 'Ten percent held by H for the Big Guy.' Now, who is—"

"No," said Lesley Wolf, cutting him off.

"What?"

"No. There is no specific criminality to ask about that."

Joe stood up and replied, "There absolutely is. If a person is receiving a percentage of ownership for someone else, that could be income to that other person. This is flat-out wrong."

Wolf heard Joe's comment, stated, "I will have to think about it," and never gave a final direction on if they could ask the question.

There was some cross talk after Lesley Wolf cut in. We argued back and forth for a while. Finally, the investigative team relented. But we weren't happy with it. For once, the FBI and the IRS were in complete agreement on something: Lesley Wolf and her team were in our way. In the time they'd been working together, Joe had noticed a few things about Wolf. Most were negative. This was probably because she seemed to be trying to hold up the investigation possibily due to a preference for Joe Biden over Donald Trump. But he had to hand it to her on one thing: she was excellent at arguing. One of her subordinates would make a suggestion, and Lesley could rip it to shreds in the time it took to blink. She was methodical in the way she took on other people. Joe had often spoken to other agents about it.

This is exactly what happened for the rest of the pre-interview meeting on December 3. Investigators would run through their outlines, letting Wolf and her DOJ colleagues know what they planned to ask. Every few lines, she'd step in and tell us we couldn't do something, especially if that something involved Joe Biden or any other member of the Biden family. By the end of the meeting, our outlines had thinned considerably. Our questions had grown far less detailed. But we still had a plan of action. Barring an act of God or another delay from high up in the Justice Department, we were finally going to move our investigation forward on December 8.

We'd planned for just about every eventuality. Gary and Joe Gordon, his counterpart at the FBI, would reach out to the Secret Service at eight o'clock in the morning on December 8 and say they were coming to interview Hunter Biden—who'd been granted Secret Service protection on December 3—as part of an official investigation. With such short notice, we figured there was no way for Hunter to wriggle out of it. We were going to get the answers we'd been looking for since 2018.

That was the plan for about five days.

Right up until it wasn't.

When you conduct an interview, especially one involving someone suspected of criminal activity, the element of surprise is crucial. If the person knows you're coming, they'll find a way to be gone when you stop by. They might use the extra time to craft lies or figure out ways to dodge the questions you're going to ask.

In the week leading up to our day of action, we'd been counting on the element of surprise. We wanted to ask Hunter Biden about his tax affairs and get real answers that he hadn't had time to spin.

We wanted the truth.

On the night before the interviews were set to take place, Gary sat in a hot tub in California, reviewing his binders of notes with a whiskey in one hand and a cigar in the other. About an hour into this prep session, he got a phone call from one of his superiors at the IRS. They let him know that FBI leadership had reached out to the Biden transition team to let them know we were coming. He was shocked—so shocked, in fact, that he almost dropped the cigar into the hot water. Over the years, he'd served many warrants and conducted many interviews. So had Joe. Neither of us had ever heard of anything like this happening. It didn't take long for us to learn that the interview was off. Instead, we'd follow a strange plan—one that was oddly, almost inexplicably, favorable to the Biden family.

The FBI gave the transition team the phone numbers of Gary and FBI supervisory special agent Gordon. In turn, the transition team let us know that *if* Hunter wanted to speak with us, he'd give us a call on the morning of December 8.

If you've been paying attention for the past few pages, we probably don't need to tell you how this went.

All morning, Gary and FBI supervisory special agent Gordon waited in a car outside Hunter Biden's house in Venice, California. No one came into the house, and no one went out. There was nothing in the driveway other than a large black Secret Service vehicle. For a long time, the phone didn't ring. When it finally did, it wasn't Hunter. It was the FBI assistant special agent in charge, Alfred Watson, who informed FBI supervisory special agent Gordon that Hunter would contact us through his attorneys.

Later that morning, once we'd all but given up on hearing anything from anyone in the Biden camp, those attorneys called. They let us know that although they would accept document requests on Hunter's behalf, their client would not be speaking with us.

All over the country, similar scenes played out. The agents who'd intended to interview one member of the Biden family were shooed away at the door of her home. The same went for the agents who wanted to interview other members of the Biden family and Hunter's business associates. We can't be sure whether FBI leadership's decision to tip off Hunter and the rest of the Bidens played a role in any of these interviews falling apart.

But then again, we can't *not* be sure either.

In the end, only one substantive interview occurred in the Hunter Biden case that day. It happened in Arkansas with none other than Rob Walker.

The IRS and FBI agents pulled up to Walker's home around 9:00 in the morning. They turned on a small, covert recording device and walked up the front drive.

A few minutes later, they were at the front door with Rob Walker. They exchanged pleasantries. Although the agents began asking their questions, Walker seemed tense, ready to walk away at any moment. The FBI special agent found a way to follow Lesley Wolf's directive without *following* it. He said, "Um, as far as the... the failed joint venture that was going to be SinoHawk, which involved Tony and James and you..."

Walker grunted in agreement.

"And Hunter."

"Mhm."

"You know, it was kind of the, um, the famous email that Tony was pointing out. Like the, the equity split."

"Sure."

"Who . . . like can you tell me your opinion of that? Like, ah, I mean, are you familiar with what I'm talking about? That email? When it's going through, you know, like, ten b, held by 'H,' you know, like . . ."

Throughout this strange, halting series of sentences, the FBI special agent had taken great pains not to say the three words that were on his mind: *the big guy*. Wolf had given us strict instructions not to mention Joe Biden. That meant no talk about "the big guy," "the vice president," "Joe," or any other monikers that would have pointed directly to the man who'd just been elected president.

Read the lines of the previous dialogue, and you'll find that the special agent followed these instructions perfectly.

But Walker knew what he meant.

"Yeah," he said.

"So, you . . ."

"Yeah, I saw that on Twitter or somethin'. Or maybe," Walker added, "when Tucker Carlson talks about it on his show."

"So, can you tell me about that?"

"It was an email. I think that maybe James was ah, wishful thinking that, ah . . . or maybe he was, ah, projecting that, you know, if this was a good relationship and if this was something that was gonna happen that, ah, if the V.P. was never gonna run . . ."

The agent grunted, encouraging Walker to keep going.

". . . just projecting that, you know, maybe at some point, he would be a piece of it but he was more just, you know, ah, you know, it . . . it . . . it looks terrible but it's not."

And there it was.

Rob Walker, who'd been directly involved in the negotiations for SinoHawk, had confirmed that Joe Biden was, in fact, "the big guy." And he'd admitted that it "looked terrible."

For the rest of the interview, the agents pressed Walker for more information on Joe Biden's involvement in his son's business dealings. They found that Joe Biden had stopped by at least one business lunch at the Four Seasons and that he had played golf with Hunter's business partners on more than one occasion. Walker expressed anger at Tony Bobulinski—his exact words were "and fuck Tony"—for putting all this out into the open.

Rob Walker's relationship with Hunter Biden was complex and evolved over time. They first met in 1999 during the Clinton administration and began collaborating professionally around 2008. Their last recorded interaction occurred in the fall of 2017 at a restaurant in Washington, D.C.'s Logan Circle area. During this meeting, Walker informed Hunter that he intended to end their business partnership primarily due to concerns about Hunter's health and issues related to the SinoHawk deal. The meeting turned tense, with raised voices and emotional exchanges, ultimately marking the end of their professional relationship.

And he'd given us key evidence.

In this, at least, going overt had been worth it. And there was no denying that we were overt now.

The subject said so himself.

—

The morning of December 9 was a big one.

Finally, after months of speculation, Hunter Biden confirmed to the public that he was under federal investigation. He confirmed it first via a statement released to his social media accounts. But the real traction came when the statement was picked up by *The Washington Post*, which became the first newspaper to report on our investigation.

The news story quoted Hunter Biden's statement, which read, in part: "I learned yesterday for the first time that the U.S. Attorney's Office in Delaware advised my legal counsel, also yesterday, that they are investigating my tax affairs. I take this matter very seriously but I am confident that a professional and objective review of these matters will demonstrate that I handled my affairs legally and appropriately, including with the benefit of professional tax advisors."

The final line was a lie, and we knew it. But we couldn't say anything publicly. Instead, we had to keep following the steps of the investigation, ensuring we didn't do anything that made us look like we were out to get Hunter Biden for political reasons. This was even more important now that the case was out in the media. We were surprised to see that "a person familiar with the case" had spoken to the *Post* on background, saying "the investigation continued during the election year but that agents took care not to take overt investigative steps as voting neared that would have made it more widely known."

We had no idea who might have spoken to the reporter. We still don't. All we were focused on was keeping our heads down and moving the case forward in the correct manner. Among the few things we'd learned during our day of action was that Hunter Biden had a storage unit in Northern Virginia. When he moved out of his Washington, D.C. offices a few years earlier, his files and business records had gone there. After the day of action, some of our agents had gone to the storage unit business and confirmed that Hunter still owned a storage unit there. Right away, Joe drafted a search warrant affidavit for the storage unit. He used a previous draft, which enabled him to get it done quickly.

In this case, speed was important. Now that Hunter Biden was aware he was under investigation, he could go into the storage unit and move all his records. He could even destroy them. That would be blatantly illegal, but everything we knew about Hunter Biden suggested he wasn't averse to doing illegal things if it served his short-term interests. Joe typed furiously all that morning, hoping to get the storage unit fully searched by the next week so we could move forward.

His email read:

> Hey Everyone –
>
> I guess I'm happy we had a draft of this. I kept the computer language in the warrant in case there are electronic devices at the site (since he literally moved his entire office) – CDs DVDs, flash drives, etc.
>
> We will work to get this approved ASAP on our end so please communicate your thoughts. I would like to possibly execute this sometime next week (I think that is reasonable given the upcoming holiday).

For more than twenty-four hours, we heard nothing.

Finally, on December 9, when we were still picking up the pieces after the failure of our day of action, Lesley Wolf wrote back. She said, "We are getting to work on this, but I want to manage expectations with regard to timing. It has to go through us, DOJ Tax, possibly OEO and definitely ED Va, who has never seen the case before. Layer in the filter requirements in the 4th Circuit and it's just not clear it's going to happen next week, even with everyone making it a priority."

Joe responded, "I completely understand and will work my hardest on my end to get you all whatever you need in getting this accomplished. Thank you all. Just wanted to put that in there as a goal for us."

He did not, in fact, completely understand. But he always tried to be nice when dealing with his colleagues, especially the ones who played a role in determining whether he'd be allowed to carry out the operations he believed were necessary to bring the case home. On December 10, shortly after a meeting of the prosecution team to decide how to move forward, Wolf called Joe. She let him know that she didn't believe getting a warrant for the storage unit was a good idea after all. He argued strongly against her position. But that was like arguing with a Category 5 hurricane. By the end of the call, he felt the very idea of a search warrant for the storage unit was seriously in jeopardy.

He hung up the phone. Joe was becoming increasingly convinced that Lesley Wolf had an agenda. He had long suspected this. Wolf and her colleagues would delay things, fail to approve requests, and generally take it easy on the Biden family under the guise of not wanting to interfere in an election. After that, it was under the guise of not wanting to interfere in a *contested* election.

But the election was over. Joe Biden was going to be inaugurated on January 20, 2021, and we had an investigation to do. If this had been any other case, there would have been a mad dash to get to that storage unit. Any other assistant U.S. attorney would have been elbowing *Joe* out of the way to get a warrant approved and see what was inside. While disagreements with prosecutors were not uncommon in Joe's experience—in fact, a case that didn't have at least a few tense moments between investigators and prosecutors was the exception rather than the rule—this was something very different. For the first time, Joe felt like he was working with a prosecutor (a *team* of prosecutors, even) who didn't want the person under investigation to get charged with a crime. Everything Wolf and her team had done since they got involved suggested this was the case.

On December 11, Wolf emailed David Weiss an article from *The New York Times*. The headline was "Material from Giuliani Spurred a Separate Justice Depart. Pursuit of Hunter Biden." Wolf seemed more worried about the way our investigation looked to the public—especially those in Democratic politics—than she was about getting the steps right internally. In the article, reporters at the *Times* attempted to prove that the allegations contained within the FD-1023 that alleged bribery of the Bidens were nothing more than political disinformation spread by Rudy Giuliani to hurt Joe Biden.

That same day, Lesley Wolf called Joe about the storage unit search warrant again, updating him on the fact that they were still waiting for approvals.

Things did not go well. Right away, Joe let her know exactly how he felt. They were taking too long to move on this. Time was running out. He believed they had a narrow window to act before Hunter Biden—or his lawyers—had the chance to sanitize whatever was inside.

Further, Joe told Wolf he'd seen records that suggested Hunter had foreign bank accounts. If they searched the storage unit, they might find evidence to confirm it. But Wolf shut that down. She told him, flat-out, that there was "no indication whatsoever" that Hunter had foreign accounts.

Joe knew better than to trust that.

However, he had a backup plan. Since they were waiting on approvals, he proposed a compromise to Wolf: they could monitor the storage unit for a month before executing a warrant. If Hunter accessed it, that would tell them something.

If he didn't, that would tell them something, too. But Wolf dismissed the idea. She called it "playing games" and said she was worried about how it might look to Hunter's attorneys. She went so far as to say that his lawyers were reputable, and they had no reason to worry.

In fact, instead of moving forward with the warrant, Wolf told him that DOJ Tax and her office management had decided to let Hunter's legal team determine what to turn over. Joe could hardly believe what he was hearing. It set him off. "That's not how we handle cases!" he exclaimed. "In any other investigation, we wouldn't be letting the subject decide what to hand over."

But Wolf was unmoved. She said she'd already heard his concerns, and if there was anything else he wanted to add, now was the time. "Every attorney involved has signed off on this plan," she said. "This is the way we're moving forward."

Joe sat there, gripping his phone, his frustration peaking. He'd given everything to this case—late nights, early mornings, weekends spent poring over documents instead of spending time with his family. And for what? Every time he tried to do his job, someone up the chain stopped him. He told Wolf that he didn't feel supported. That it seemed like the assistant U.S. attorneys were dragging their feet because they were afraid of litigation. Afraid of politics. Afraid of doing their jobs.

That was the moment Wolf lost her patience. Her voice sharpened. She told Joe she had a problem with what he was implying. That he'd had plenty of influence on this case. That she often went along with his recommendations, even when she didn't agree with them.

She wasn't done. If Joe had a problem, she said, maybe they should take it to upper management and figure out how to "resolve" it.

Joe took a breath. He hadn't wanted the call to go this way. He apologized for offending her—but held firm. He wasn't making this up. He was telling her what he saw, what he knew.

Wolf didn't budge. She said she'd already gone out of her way to accommodate the investigation, even arranging for Hunter to be interviewed through the Secret Service. And she let Joe know something else. He didn't understand, she said, how much effort it had taken just to get this far.

Joe let that sit for a second. He told her he didn't want a bad working relationship. But he also wasn't going to sit back and let politics dictate an investigation.

He had support. His assistant special agent in charge and special agent in charge—they were with him on this.

Wolf exhaled. "I'll think about it," she said. "I'll bring it to the other attorneys."

But then she added something else.

"I don't think you're right."

In the end, Wolf ended up going around David Weiss's back by tipping off the defense counsel about the plan, which we called "Joe's Plan" around the office. Joe had long had a feeling that it was Wolf, and not David Weiss, who was really in charge of the case. Now he had his first solid evidence of that.

No one had suggested that Joe might lose his job over this. But it certainly felt like that was on the table. At the very least, he was afraid that if they took things to upper management, he might be reprimanded or passed over for promotions. He'd seen Lesley Wolf argue during prosecution meetings, and he had no doubt that if it came down to it, he'd probably lose a battle with her and her colleagues. It didn't matter how much evidence—how many documented missed opportunities, notes on calls, and other proof of stonewalling—he brought to whatever meeting they ended up having.

And Joe couldn't afford to jeopardize his career. After so many missed days taking care of his mother, David had lost his job as a personal trainer, leaving him without an income or health insurance. Partly because of this, and partly because they were genuinely in love at the time, he and Joe decided to get married. They had a small ceremony at the house on December 5, 2020, just three days before the day of action on the Hunter Biden case. The whole time, Joe felt phantom vibrations in his suit pocket, wondering if he was going to get an email or a phone call with bad news from work. There was no honeymoon.

By this point, Gary was also fed up. It got to the point where we'd have calls with the full team and then break off for a separate call to say some variation of "Can you *believe* what's going on here?" back and forth until we were both blue in the face. It was becoming increasingly clear that although this investigation would eventually end, it probably wasn't going to end with an indictment of Hunter Biden for tax crimes. The people running the show—who, it bears repeating, were not the people who were *supposed* to be running the show—would make sure of that.

And now, to make matters worse, we were no longer operating in secrecy. Any mistakes we made would show up in the pages of *The New York Times* the very next day. Every political reporter in America wanted to know what we were doing. The media requests were piling up—so much so that we began every prosecution team meeting with a list of inquiries we'd gotten from newspapers and cable news networks. And Hunter Biden, who had often admitted that he held "a grudge" and was willing to do terrible things to get back at people, was now aware that he was under investigation—and that we were the ones investigating him. Although the Biden family did not have a reputation in the mainstream press as vindictive fighters who often sought to crush their enemies by any means necessary, the messages we'd seen behind the scenes proved that this was definitely the case.

Whatever happened next, it was going to be a fight—with the Biden family, Hunter's attorneys, and, apparently, our own bosses. We prepared as best we could.

But we had no idea how bad things were about to get.

PART TWO

OUT IN THE OPEN

SIX

THE FIGHT TO MAKE THE CASE

ON THE AFTERNOON of January 20, 2021, Joe Biden was inaugurated as the forty-sixth president of the United States. As he spoke on the steps of the Capitol building, several members of his family sat behind him along with every living former president (other than Donald Trump, who didn't attend) and dignitaries from all over the country.

Hunter Biden sat in the crowd, a little removed from everyone else.

Things were going to change in the country. Joe Biden assured us of this in his Inaugural Address, which centered on themes of hope and unity. The days of corruption and self-dealing that Democrats had complained about during President Trump's term were now behind us. During an interview with CNN's Jake Tapper on the campaign trail, Joe Biden had been asked about rumors that President Trump was considering "a wave of preemptive pardons" for members of his family. In response, Biden had said, "[That] concerns me in terms of what kind of precedent it sets and the way the rest of the world looks at us as a nation of law and justice. You're not going to see in our administration that kind of approach to pardons ... It's going to be a totally different way in which we approach the justice system."

The message of Biden's Inaugural Address largely supported this message. Under his administration, the wheels of justice were going to turn smoothly. It wouldn't matter who was being investigated or what the charges were. Given our experience, of course, we were skeptical about this from the beginning. Over the past few years we'd seen obstruction of justice, and none of it had come from the Trump White House. It had come, rather, from our superiors at the Department of Justice, the IRS, and the FBI, many of whom seemed to tremble at the mention of Joe Biden's name. And now, instead of being a candidate for the presidency, Joe Biden was the head of the executive branch. Technically, that meant he was the boss of everyone investigating his son, us included. If you went by his rhetoric, you'd believe that he wasn't going to abuse that power. But if you went by his actions and the secret messages that went back and forth about him among members of the Biden family, you might not be so sure.

About two weeks after the inauguration, the Department of Justice announced that David Weiss, who'd been appointed by President Trump, would remain in his post to oversee the Hunter Biden investigation. They seemed to understand that removing Weiss and replacing him with someone else—especially someone from Delaware—would smack of favoritism and corruption. Given our experience on the case, we weren't sure just how much effect Weiss would have on the day-to-day operations of the case. But it was good to see the administration making the right gestures in public.

In February, Merrick Garland appeared before the Senate Judiciary Committee for a hearing. Joe Biden had nominated Garland as attorney general almost as soon as Biden won the election, and Democrats had celebrated. They remembered that Barack Obama had nominated Garland to the Supreme Court only to have his nomination torpedoed by Mitch McConnell and other Senate Republicans who refused to give him a hearing. It seemed that the AG nomination was a kind of payback for all Garland had endured. During this hearing, the subject of the Biden family came up a few times. Without fail, Garland said the right things. He assured senators that David Weiss would have all the independence in the world; he would be able to bring charges wherever he wanted and follow up on any investigative leads he wanted to.

A few days before his confirmation hearing, Representative Ken Buck of Colorado sent Garland a letter urging him to either keep Weiss in place or replace him with a special counsel. The administration seemed to have gotten ahead of this. But for the first time, it had been suggested in public that a special counsel might be necessary in this case. Unlike traditional prosecutors, special counsels operate with a greater degree of independence from the Department of Justice, have the authority to investigate and prosecute cases with minimal direct oversight from DOJ leadership, and are typically appointed to handle cases where the Justice Department may have a conflict of interest. Presidents face serious repercussions for firing them, as such an action can trigger accusations of obstruction of justice and political backlash, sometimes leading to congressional investigations or even impeachment proceedings.

But we weren't there yet.

For the time being, we were going to keep working the case under David Weiss, Lesley Wolf, and the rest of the prosecutors who'd been holding us up for nearly three years. To make matters worse, there had been even more changes in management. When

IRS special agent in charge Kelly Jackson retired, special agent in charge Darrell Waldon took over. This didn't bode well for us.

But we were going to hope for the best.

—

This strategy didn't work for long.

On March 2, Gary met with Darrell Waldon and Mike Batdorf, the special agent in charge and the director of field operations at the IRS, to discuss how the case had been going. Given the new political realities and the fact that the case was not moving, he raised the possibility with them of blowing the whistle. Waldon and Batdorf recoiled at the suggestion.

To be clear, Gary didn't want to embarrass the agency publicly or make himself a public figure unless it was absolutely necessary. First, he wanted to raise the issue within the IRS following all the proper steps and working through the chain of command. On May 3, he sent up a sensitive case report that read: "This investigation has been hampered and slowed by claims of potential election meddling. Through interviews and review of evidence obtained, it appears there may be campaign finance criminal violations. Wolf stated on the last prosecution team meeting that she did not want any of the agents to look into the allegation. She cited a need to focus on the 2014 tax year, that we could not yet prove an allegation beyond a reasonable doubt, and that she does not want to include their Public Integrity Unit because they would take authority away from her. We do not agree with her obstruction on this matter."

Joe had attempted to keep working the case, now keeping in close contact with Gary. On April 27, 2021, he flew to Los Angeles to conduct an interview with Jeffrey Gelfound, the man who'd prepared Hunter Biden's late tax returns. During that interview, it became even more clear that Hunter claimed many deductions that were improper.

On June 14, investigators interviewed one of the many escorts who'd shown up in Hunter's business files. The story was almost too strange to believe. According to her, the escort—whose name we still aren't at liberty to reveal—met Hunter on the app Telegram, and she was paid $800 an hour to spend time with him.

During their first meeting, she asked Hunter to provide identification, as was standard procedure. He presented an ID that she described as "weird" and not a California-issued identification card. When she requested a second form of ID, someone communicating with Hunter via cell phone instructed him to provide another form of identification, which he did—a "global ID." During their time together, Hunter told her that his father was the vice president and even suggested she google his name. When she showed no interest, he then displayed a picture of his father with President Barack Obama, which frightened her.

After she left the location, she returned to her apartment and told a friend what had happened. Her friend warned her, saying, "You have no idea who you're dealing with." Following this, she deleted Hunter's number.

And that was only one story.

That August, after a few more months of digging, Joe sent Lesley Wolf an email regarding his plans to interview several more people. Among them were a former employee, previous business partners, and individuals connected to the 2018 expenditures.

He wrote: "Attached are ▮▮▮▮▮▮▮. I plan on doing ▮▮▮▮▮▮▮ Monday Afternoon / Evening (9/13) in DC (With Christine) and ▮▮▮▮▮▮▮ on Tuesday (9/14) with Sue in Maryland. Please let me know if you have any questions."

After weeks of radio silence, Wolf wrote back:

I do not think that you are going to be able to do these interviews as planned. ▆▆▆ require approval from Tax Division. At present, Jack and Mark are racing to get the EWC motion onto Stuart's desk for approval before he leaves town for a week, along with the approval for the Mesires ▆▆▆ . Both of these items are higher priority and we can't pull time and attention away to move these ▆▆▆ through. Appreciate that you are trying to stay active (and do some travel before year end), but we will be able to get these interviews ▆▆▆ done when we have a little more breathing room. I did leave a message for Lunden's lawyer this morning—he was in court, but I anticipate talking to him tomorrow and expect that can get scheduled for the near future.

Around tomorrow if you want to chat on this.

Joe was incensed. This time, he didn't try to hide it. He replied:

OK — I had planned stuff like this weeks in advance to prevent this from happening. I had brought up these interviews on multiple occasions dating back to August 18th, and now we are being prevented from doing it 4 days before. This is making it difficult for me in doing my job. I don't understand why DOJ-Tax Senior Management is needing to approve ▆▆▆ and/or witness interviews and maybe this is a conversation that needs to be had at a higher level.

I can push these interviews off, just know that I am trying to do as much as I can to plan and get the tasks handed down to me accomplished in a timely manner, in effort to ultimately finish the pros report.

I discussed with Mark that the interviews we have planned for the end of the month should be a priority as they relate to a former employee, previous business partners, and some of the 2018 Expenditures. I will have ▆▆▆ for

THE FIGHT TO MAKE THE CASE

those interviews in California to the pros team by early next week, so we don't have this issue again.

If you would like to talk, please call me. I'm available all afternoon.

—Joe

Immediately after getting the emails, Gary reached out to Jason Poole at DOJ Tax—the person who allegedly needed to approve his interview requests—to make sure this was really the case. He wrote that he had agents ready to travel and conduct interviews. But he didn't hear back from Poole in time to set them up.

As time went on and the delays piled up, Joe began opening up to his colleagues about how frustrated he was. On September 20, shortly after an attorney at DOJ Tax—who, unlike many of his colleagues, had always been good about moving things along—submitted a few document requests for him, Joe wrote, "You are the man!! Thank you. I'll fill you in tomorrow on my issues. I'm almost at the end of my rope and I'm sick of fighting to do what's right." That night, after emailing a few other investigators, Joe wrote to one of the his senior leaders at the IRS. He said, "I'm almost at the end of my rope and I think I'm at the point again where I need your help. I have a ton of interviews and travel planned and scheduled for the next 3 months, keeping on a timeline is extremely important and I don't want this to continue to be a problem. I don't mind the questions from management, but it feels like they are not listening to me."

Looking back, this seems a little dramatic. But every word of it was true. After all, there were only so many times you could smash into the brick wall of bureaucracy without venting your concerns, even in writing. As Joe continued to try to get his search warrants and interview requests approved, speculation about whether Hunter would ever face a serious trial for his crimes mounted. On September 21, a producer from CNN called the communications office at the IRS and said that his news organization had an email from Hunter Biden—one we hadn't yet seen. In this email, apparently, Hunter had said that he expected all this "stuff" (meaning the investigation into his taxes) to go away as soon as his dad became president.

It was our policy not to give these things much thought. We did take a few minutes at the beginning of every prosecution team meeting to discuss media inquiries, but more often than not we decided to do nothing. A lot of the time, the stories that these people were writing never materialized. We figured this would be similar. But as soon as Joe heard about this Hunter Biden email, his ears pricked up. The only reason Hunter would be discussing this, Joe knew, was because someone had floated a plea bargain to him. In other words, Hunter seemed to believe that someone was going to offer to make him a deal. The context of the email suggested that he wasn't going to take that deal.

The next day, during a meeting of the prosecution team, Joe asked Lesley Wolf directly whether Hunter had been offered a plea agreement. She said he hadn't been. In fact, according to Wolf, we weren't even at the point where we could file charges, let alone discuss a way for Hunter to potentially *avoid* those charges. No one needed to tell Joe that, of course. He still had a long list of witnesses and documents he'd need to review before anyone could bring real charges.

All throughout the fall of 2021, we worked to gather these materials. There were more bumps in the road, which was no longer a surprise. On September 24, we were told that no document requests could be served until DOJ Tax approved them. In October, Wolf denied our requests to interview some of President Biden's adult grandchildren who'd received payments from Hunter. She said that doing so would get them into "hot water." But there were some interviews we did manage to get. We reinterviewed Hunter Biden's accountants, for instance, who clarified a few important questions about his tax returns. And we spoke to Rob Walker a second time, who told us that funds from Chinese energy conglomerate CEFC had been directed to multiple accounts at Hunter Biden's request, including those belonging to members of his family. Walker confirmed that Hunter had instructed him to send money to his sister-in-law Liz Secundy's account, though Walker did not know why. He also revealed that at least one payment was directed to Hunter Biden's daughter Finnegan, though he claimed he was unaware of that fact at the time. Additionally, Walker described the $3 million CEFC payment as a "thank you" for introductions made to various energy and infrastructure contacts, and he acknowledged that he had split those funds with Hunter and business partner James Gilliar.

On the strength of this evidence, the full prosecution team finally began settling on the exact charges we wanted to pursue in October 2021. We determined that we would recommend to charge Hunter Biden with two felonies (for tax years 2014 and 2018) as well as misdemeanors for some tax years. Additional misdemeanor charges were proposed for 2019 and potentially 2020 based on his failure to timely file and pay his taxes during those years.

Once we'd decided what charges to bring, it fell to Joe to compile a special agent report that we could send up the chain. These reports, which often run to more than one thousand pages, contain all the evidence we'd gathered throughout our investigation as well as commentary and analysis. Writing one was like putting together ten college term papers. Joe worked on this one all throughout Thanksgiving, pecking at the keys of his laptop in the living room of his house while family gathered inside. Finally, after many hours of working, it was done. A few weeks later, he got an email from Lesley Wolf to thank the prosecution team for all their work on the case. It read:

> Team,
>
> I am about to head out for leave through the new year, but before doing so, just wanted to take a moment to thank you for all of your work on this investigation over the last year. We've been able to accomplish so much only because of our efforts as a group (with extra credit to Joe Z, of course) and look forward to seeing where 2022 takes us. Your professionalism, dedication, and at times much needed senses of humor are greatly appreciated.
>
> If you need me over the holidays, I will look at email on occasion, but if you really need me, the ▮▮▮▮▮▮ cell is the way to go. In the meantime, I wish you all happy, healthy holidays and a wonderful new year.

Reading it, Joe felt a little of the frustration that had been mounting over the past few years melt away. With almost every investigation, he knew, people butted heads. Investigators got frustrated that management wasn't letting them chase down certain leads, and management got frustrated that investigators were too gung ho. For a moment, it seemed that the Sportsman case might go down in history as just another one of these cases—albeit one that was a little more strained than usual, given the political implications and the strange circumstances surrounding the Department of Justice at the time. After all, things hadn't been tense *all* the time.

The implication of Wolf's email was clear. We were almost at the end of the line. And that was a good thing. All throughout the investigation, we'd been aware that the statute of limitations on the 2014 case would soon expire. As a rule, the IRS has six years to charge someone with most tax violations; after that, the statute of limitations runs out and there's nothing we can do. Although there were moments when we suspected our superiors were attempting to get us past that deadline to save the Biden family from embarrassment, we'd never been able to prove it.

Still, the constant delays made us wonder. The deadline was looming, and there were still many opportunities for things to get derailed.

On January 27, 2022, Gary signed Joe's special agent report. The month prior, Joe sent it up the chain for review by the IRS's criminal tax counsel.

This is a step that all our cases go through. The criminal tax counsel, or "CT counsel" for short, reviews the special agent report and looks for any potential legal issues. In essence, the CT counsel serves in an advisory capacity. They give each charge a rating of "green light," which means it's totally good to go, down to "red light," which means it probably won't hold up in court. "Yellow light" means we're still good to go, but we might run into some problems in court. As our special agent report made its way through these levels of approval, we checked in often. Every time we did, the line attorney at the CT counsel's office—a bright, competent lawyer named Christy Steinbrunner, who'd been with us almost from the beginning—said she was writing a memorandum that would give us mostly green lights. The only yellow lights were for the earlier tax years.

This was understandable. From the start of the investigation, we'd understood that once we brought these charges to court, a jury might look sympathetically on the Hunter Biden of 2014 and 2015—the guy who seemed to be grieving the death of his older brother sliding further into drug and alcohol addiction. We could imagine a world in which the jury would vote to take it easy on him because of all he'd been going through. But the other tax years seemed solid. They would hold up in court, and a jury would probably vote to convict.

After the soft green light from Christy, we waited.

And then waited some more, as usual.

Sixty days passed, which was a significant amount of time to wait for a review of a special agent report. When Joe checked in with Christy, she let him know that *her* report—which, we assumed, recommended green lights on all charges and maybe two yellow lights—had gone up to her superiors. Finally, after the sixty-day deadline had passed, someone at the CT counsel's office contacted Joe's co–case agent, and let her know that the five-member review panel above her had agreed with all charges. They planned to issue a "concur" memo on everything. Although the "concur" opinion wasn't necessary to move forward with the case—we could do it no matter what the CT counsel said—it was always good to have one.

We waited some more, pleased to finally be expecting good news.

Then the memo came down.

As soon as Joe opened the document and scanned through it, he knew something was wrong. Amid all the dense, bureaucratic language was a word that made his heart sink: *nonconcur—to all recommended counts in the report.*

The CT counsel's office—or, rather, someone above them—had intervened, and now we were being told not to pursue charges. When Joe checked in with Christy, she was almost as confused as he was about why the change occurred. But at least she knew what happened. According to Christy, she had sent her report up the chain with a recommendation to concur, and her superiors had written back asking whether that was *really* what she wanted to do. There was some language in her report, they said, that suggested she might want to give all these charges red lights.

So that's what happened.

The official recommendation of the IRS's lawyer was that Hunter Biden should not be charged for tax crimes. And they claimed that even Christy had told them this was the right thing to do.

Luckily, we didn't have to listen. And we usually don't. About 90 percent of the time, when the CT counsel's office—which operates out of an abundance of caution—gives us negative advisory opinions, we'll still try to make the case. We decided to move forward with the Sportsman case anyway, moving it through to its final stages. Gary transmitted Joe's special agent report up to Darrell Waldon, their IRS special agent in charge, and worked to get it over to DOJ Tax before the statute of limitations for the 2014 tax year was set to expire.

In the end, we recommended six felony charges—three for false returns and three for evasion of assessment—for the years 2014, 2018, and 2019, along with five misdemeanor charges for failure to timely file and pay from 2015 through 2019. We were confident that these charges would hold up in court just like our CT counsel had been (until, for mysterious reasons, she supposedly wasn't).

Unlike many other agencies that charge people with crimes, the IRS gives people plenty of chances to explain themselves. We send letters. We do interviews. We allow people to amend tax returns that have been fraudulently or incorrectly filed. And as long as they do that, there's a chance that we won't pursue criminal charges.

When things go as far down the line as they did in the Sportsman case, we give our subjects one final chance to make their case before things go to court. Lawyers for the taxpayer are permitted to engage in what's known as a "taxpayer conference," during which they can present evidence to the DOJ as to why their client should not be prosecuted for tax crimes. Over the course of our careers, we've seen taxpayer conferences go either way. Sometimes, evidence not known to the investigators is presented backing up the taxpayer's defense of why they shouldn't be charged—and sometimes this can sway the DOJ not to charge a taxpayer.

The first taxpayer conference with Hunter Biden's attorneys occurred on March 14, 2022. We weren't invited. And when we *asked* to be invited, we were turned down. During this meeting, Hunter's attorneys attempted to convince the DOJ that we didn't have a case. Meanwhile, we continued to conduct interviews and follow up on investigative leads, wanting to build the strongest case possible. Around this time, we also sent all our communications regarding the case up to the U.S. Attorney's Office in Delaware, which needed them for the discovery process as a result of our recommended charges. This was relatively normal, and we'd done it in other cases. Of course, our communications in *this* case contained many emails back and forth in which we had discussed the various delays we experienced, many of which were sent in the heat of the moment. We didn't think the U.S. Attorney's Office would be thrilled to see them. But right now, it was hard to focus on anything other than getting the case over the finish line.

In the press, Hunter Biden and his allies attempted to sway the public to their way of thinking. Unlike us, they didn't have a requirement to keep the details of the case secret. It was no surprise that just a few days after the first taxpayer conference, a story appeared in *The New York Times* about our cases titled "Hunter Biden Paid Tax Bill, but Broad Federal Investigation Continues." The first two paragraphs of this story, which relied heavily on the testimony of Biden allies, read:

> In the year after he disclosed a federal investigation into his "tax affairs" in late 2020, President Biden's son, Hunter Biden, paid off a significant tax liability, even as a grand jury continued to gather evidence in a wide-ranging examination of his international business dealings, according to people familiar with the case.
>
> Mr. Biden's failure to pay all his taxes has been a focus of the ongoing Justice Department investigation. While wiping out his liability does not preclude criminal charges against him, the payment could make it harder for prosecutors to win a conviction or a long sentence for tax-related offenses, according to tax law experts, since juries and judges tend to be more sympathetic to defendants who have paid their bills.

Every day we delayed, the chances increased that public opinion—and therefore the pool of potential jurors—would come to sympathize more with Hunter Biden. And that was assuming that the statute of limitations on the 2014 tax year didn't expire. Luckily, Hunter Biden's attorneys agreed to sign an agreement that would extend the statute of limitations for a period of time, to potentially be extended again, while they continued to make their case to prosecutors.

Meanwhile, the case made its way up the ranks at the U.S. Attorney's Office in Washington, D.C.—the jurisdiction where, by all accounts, we were going to try to bring some of the charges. But doing so would ultimately require the approval of the U.S. attorney for the District of Columbia, Matthew Graves, who had been appointed by President Biden just a few months earlier. Given that the investigation centered on the president's son, this represented a clear conflict of interest for Graves. In late March, DOJ Tax and the Delaware U.S. Attorney's Office presented the case to Graves's office. We requested to attend this briefing, just to ensure the evidence was presented accurately and in full context, but we were denied. That was frustrating—especially given how many times we'd seen prosecutors, through no fault of their own, get key facts wrong in complicated cases like this. Someone like Joe, who knew the case inside and out, could've made sure everything was explained clearly. But every time we asked to be in the room, we were shut out.

Shortly after that meeting, a DOJ Tax attorney named Mark Daly called Joe to say that the D.C. U.S. Attorney's Office was feeling optimistic about the case. Around the same time, on March 31, the White House communications director was asked during a press briefing about Hunter's corrupt business dealings. A reporter asked, "During the last presidential debate, then Vice President Biden was asked if there was anything inappropriate or unethical about his son's relationships, business dealings in China and/or Ukraine. The president said, 'Nothing was unethical.' He went on to say, 'My son has not made money in terms of this thing about, what you're talking about, China.' Does the White House stand by that comment that the then vice president made?" The press secretary replied, "We absolutely stand by the president's comment. And I would point you to the reporting on this, which reference statements that we made at the time that we gave to *The Washington Post*, who worked on this story."

THE FIGHT TO MAKE THE CASE

This was a lie. The documents and emails we had uncovered during our investigation, as well as the interviews we'd conducted, could *prove* that it was a lie. But we were barred from disclosing any of that material publicly. The press, on the other hand, was free to speculate. They were also free to take the narrative of Hunter Biden's lawyers as fact. The only way to get the truth out, for now at least, was a public trial, just like the dozens of other public trials that had resulted from our cases.

But the chances of that happening were diminishing fast. Joe soon got another phone call from Mark Daly, an attorney at DOJ Tax who'd helped present the case to D.C. In a situation that was eerily similar to the one that had played out with Christy at the CT counsel's office, Mark let Joe know that attorneys from D.C. not only said that they weren't going to help us charge the case in their district, but that they also didn't think that we had a viable tax case. Once again, everything had been good—the evidence, the jurisdiction, and the timing—until it wasn't. We never learned *why* the attorneys from the office, including U.S. attorney Matthew Graves, didn't want to charge the case in D.C. They just let us know it wouldn't be happening. We couldn't help but wonder if the White House press briefing impacted the decision.

The case, for now, was in legal limbo. We had all the evidence we needed to charge, but we didn't have a venue to bring those charges. We also didn't have a prosecutor willing to take on the Biden family in court, largely because doing so might make them the target of political retribution. Their answer, as usual, was to do nothing.

Meanwhile, the Biden camp built their case in public. Chief of Staff Ron Klain said on ABC's *The Week* that President Biden was confident Hunter had not broken the law. On April 26, during a second taxpayer conference, Hunter Biden's lawyers presented a hundred-slide PowerPoint to prosecutors trying to dissuade them from bringing charges. We requested to be present at this meeting so we could rebut any false claims and provide necessary background information, but we were denied again. We were, in fact, denied permission to attend *any* meetings with Hunter Biden's defense counsel.

At the very moment this second taxpayer conference was happening, Attorney General Merrick Garland testified in front of a Senate Appropriations subcommittee. During this hearing, Senator Bill Hagerty of Tennessee said, "The matter of the Hunter Biden investigation [has] received a great deal of press, but I want to ask you how the communications have worked within your department and with the White House on this. First, have you been briefed on the Hunter Biden investigation matter yourself?"

Garland replied: "The Hunter Biden investigation, as I said even in my own confirmation hearing, is being supervised by and run by the United States attorney for the District of Delaware."

"I'm aware of that," Senator Hagerty said. "But he reports to you."

"He is supervising the investigation, and I'm not at liberty to talk about internal Justice Department deliberations, but he is in charge of that investigation. There will not be interference of any political or improper kind."

Pressing on, Senator Hagerty asked if any senior officials in the Justice Department were being briefed on the investigation, and Garland attempted to duck the question. Senator Hagerty continued: "Earlier this month, White House chief of staff, Ron Klain, stated on national television that quote, 'the president is confident that his son didn't break the law,' and the White House communications director said that President Biden maintains his position that his son did nothing that was unethical. This is on national television. The president has already told his subordinates, clearly—these are people that he can fire at will—that he and his family did nothing wrong. How can the American people be confident that his administration is conducting a serious investigation?"

"Because we put the investigation in the hands of a Trump appointee," the attorney general said.

In closing, Senator Hagerty said, "Well, I think the observation here is terribly critical, because there's an obvious conflict of interest here because, if those who are investigating the Biden family and their enterprise can be fired by the head of the family who's being investigated—that is, Joe Biden can fire the attorney general in Delaware [U.S. attorney for the District of Delaware]—he can have an impact on all of your staffing."

Gary didn't watch this hearing live. He only heard about it afterward on the news. When he did, he was glad to see that someone was asking the right questions about the investigation into Hunter Biden. While Gary had worked investigations for the IRS that involved giant sums of money before—not to mention criminal taxpayers who had a lot of political and legal weight to throw around—this was brand new to him. Even though he was about seven layers down in the pecking order at the IRS, Joe Biden was his boss. As of January 20, 2021, Joe Biden was *everyone's* boss. And for the past four years now, we had been attempting to bring a case against the boss's son.

In a sense, it was no wonder things had ended up in a stalemate. Everyone around us was terrified that if they dug too deep into Hunter Biden's finances—especially given the increasingly intense public scrutiny of our work—they would face retribution. Maybe this would mean being fired. Maybe it would mean being denied promotions. No one knew for sure what would happen because we were in uncharted territory. And we hadn't yet reached the point where associates of the Biden family were making direct threats.

But we were going to get there very soon.

The only option to move forward in a serious way seemed to be breaking the chain of command and appointing a special counsel. On May 9, Senators Chuck Grassley and Ron Johnson, who'd become some of the most strident defenders of our work in public, wrote to David Weiss with questions. They wanted to know, first and foremost, whether any employees in Weiss's office had been recused from the Hunter Biden case. They also wanted to know whether he had discussed the need for a special counsel.

Later that month, Gary got a call from Joe Gordon at the FBI. He and his team had witnessed the same obstruction from the DOJ that we had. He said his leadership believed they should push for a special counsel, who'd have certain protections that David Weiss didn't currently have. Near the end of the call, he wondered why leadership at the IRS wasn't trying to do the same thing.

Shortly after the call, Gary went to one of his superiors with the question.

This person paused and looked away, seeming to think about it. For a second, Gary had some hope. Maybe getting a special counsel required nothing other than asking for one. But the person he was speaking to came back with a nonchalant shake of the head.

"You know what?" he said. "I wouldn't even know how to do that."

And that, for the moment, was that.

SEVEN

CAN WE ASK FOR A SPECIAL COUNSEL?

WHEN MOST PEOPLE hear the phrase "special counsel," they think controversy. That's because by the time an investigation gets to the point at which a special counsel is appointed there have usually been at least some reports of wrongdoing or political bias. The appointment itself signals that something has become too big, too politically sensitive, or too legally complex to remain within the usual channels. It suggests, in other words, that the case has crossed a threshold—from a standard investigation into something that could shake institutions, implicate powerful figures, or test the limits of justice.

The concept of a special prosecutor dates back nearly 150 years. The first such appointment came in 1875 when President Ulysses S. Grant's administration became embroiled in the Whiskey Ring scandal—a massive fraud in which distillers and government officials conspired to siphon millions of dollars in liquor taxes from the U.S. Treasury. To restore public trust, Grant appointed John B. Henderson as special prosecutor to root out the corruption. It was an early recognition that, when the executive branch was implicated in wrongdoing, an independent investigator was necessary to ensure accountability.

That precedent took hold. When the Teapot Dome scandal erupted in the 1920s—one of the most infamous cases of government corruption in American history—special prosecutors were again called upon to investigate. This time, it was a bribery scheme involving government-controlled oil reserves and top cabinet officials, including the secretary of the interior. The scandal led to prison sentences for high-ranking figures and cemented the idea that in moments of profound government malfeasance, only an independent investigation could maintain the public's faith in the justice system.

The modern era of special counsels began in the wake of Watergate. When President Richard Nixon's administration was implicated in a sweeping cover-up of illegal political espionage, the Justice Department, under intense public pressure, appointed Archibald Cox as special prosecutor in 1973. Cox's pursuit of White House tapes led to the infamous Saturday Night Massacre, in which Nixon ordered the firing of the special prosecutor—a move that backfired spectacularly and hastened Nixon's downfall. Watergate fundamentally reshaped public expectations for how government investigations should be handled in cases involving the highest levels of power.

In response, Congress passed the Ethics in Government Act, which formalized the role of an independent counsel—an investigator legally protected from executive interference. That law gave rise to perhaps the most famous special prosecutor of the twentieth century: Ken Starr. Appointed in the 1990s, Starr was originally tasked with investigating a failed Arkansas real estate deal known as Whitewater, but ended up pursuing charges related to President Bill Clinton's affair with Monica Lewinsky.

The investigation, which led to Clinton's impeachment by the House of Representatives, demonstrated how politically explosive these appointments could become.

The law that created Starr's role expired in 1999, but the Justice Department retained the ability to appoint special counsels under its own authority. That led to Robert Mueller's appointment in 2017 to investigate Russian interference in the 2016 presidential election and possible coordination with the Trump campaign. The Mueller probe, which resulted in numerous indictments but stopped short of criminal charges against the sitting president, highlighted both the power and the limitations of these investigations.

Unlike their predecessors under the Independent Counsel Act, today's special counsels answer to the attorney general rather than operating as free agents. But the purpose remains the same: when an investigation reaches a point where political pressure, public scrutiny, or legal complexity demands an independent arbiter, a special counsel is called in.

By April 2022, we believed we had long passed the point at which a special counsel was necessary. But no one knew quite how to go about it. While we scrambled to figure it out, prosecutors continued to have meetings with Hunter Biden's lawyers. Then even those began to get delayed. On May 13, Gary learned that a third taxpayer conference with Hunter's legal team that had been scheduled for that day had been put off until the end of the month.

He wrote:

Mike/Darrell,

We learned today that the new tentative date for the 3rd taxpayer conference (that we believed was scheduled for next week) is tentatively planned for 5/31. I stress tentatively.

> As a result of the new time frame, I wanted to ask if you thought it may be better to request to present to Jason Poole/David Weiss in advance of that meeting. It made sense to wait when the meeting was next week but the delay might change your mind.
>
> This tactic . . . to move things down the road backing us up against a statute . . . appears to be purposeful at this point.
>
> We will make ourselves available when you determine the preferable time frame to offer to present.
>
> Thanks and have a great weekend.

This was the first time Gary had accused DOJ, in writing, of attempting to delay the investigation on purpose. But given the rapidly increasing chances that the case would never come before a judge, he figured it was important to document all the missteps.

At some point during the taxpayer conferences—we don't know *which* point, because we weren't there—Hunter's lawyers objected to some of the charges involving the 2014 and 2015 tax years. Prosecutors then grew skittish about bringing charges relating to these years and asked investigators to reexamine the evidence surrounding them. Joe sprang right into action along with the FBI forensic accountant, once again combing through all the emails and messages they'd gotten from their warrants and searches of the Hunter Biden laptop over the years. This time, they found something new: multiple emails that laid out the scheme in order for Hunter to divert his Burisma income, and in turn, not pay taxes on that income.

Joe presented this new information to the prosecutors with pride. It seemed to address all their concerns. But they still weren't convinced. During a phone call, when prosecutors said they were still hesitant about charging that year, Joe discussed the scheme in detail with the prosecutor. DOJ Tax attorney Jack Morgan countered by saying Hunter Biden's lawyers had put forward a good defense.

"I get that, Jack," Joe said. "But I don't think you're looking at the evidence appropriately."

A chill came over that call.

Morgan went silent for a moment, then said, "Do we have a problem here, Joe? Are you questioning my ethics? Are you questioning my integrity?"

They went back and forth, walking things back and returning to a baseline. Joe said he wasn't questioning anyone's integrity. What he *was* doing was making sure everyone understood the evidence as well as he did—which, again, was the reason he'd been on this case for so long in the first place. He'd traveled on weekends to interview sources, spent countless hours poring over documents, and done so much research that he practically could have re-created Hunter Biden's tax returns from memory.

These arguments did very little to sway anyone.

On June 15, we attended a "tax summit" at the headquarters of the Department of Justice in Washington, D.C. Everyone who had a hand in the case was present: DOJ Tax attorneys; David Weiss and his colleagues at the Delaware U.S. Attorney's Office; several special agents at the FBI, as well as their leadership; and a few agents who'd worked the case at the IRS. It was the first time this many people had been together in the same room for a single purpose. And that purpose was deciding how to respond to the arguments that Hunter Biden's attorneys had put forward in his defense. In what was beginning to feel like a strange version of the film *Groundhog Day*, we presented our evidence, and prosecutors pushed back on it. Apparently, they were happy with the defense Hunter's lawyers had put forward.

We had at least one person on our side: FBI special agent in charge Tom Sobocinski. He interrupted the meeting multiple times to say there was more than enough evidence to bring tax charges. During breaks in the meeting, he pulled us aside and said, "If these were FBI charges, we'd have brought them already."

The next week, David Weiss emailed us with a request, writing:

> Joe/Gary,
>
> Thanks very much for taking the time to meet last week and to present additional information regarding the case. I am always appreciative and mindful of the extraordinary effort the team, and specifically SA Ziegler, have put into the case.
>
> At the conclusion of our meeting, you asked about additional investigative steps or work to be done by CI in advance of any decision on charges. Having further considered this, I believe it would be helpful to me and the team to have a clear understanding of tax loss associated with the case, both in total and on an annual basis. I know this calculation has shifted a bit over the last couple of months as we have discovered new evidence, ▮▮▮▮▮, and re-examined tax filings. In order to more fully inform our charging decision, I would like to see where the calculations are at this time.
>
> My understanding is that Joe has done the tax comps to date. Certainly, there is no issue with the work he has done. But I also know from other cases that a revenue agent is typically assigned and undertakes responsibility for, in essence, redoing the returns based on the raw data and analysis of flow through entities. In this case, that analysis should include all of Sportsman's returns as well as RSB's

and Archer's 1040s. Ultimately, I think it would be helpful to have a revenue agent perform this task, for two reasons. First, this is often, if not usually, the way this is done and we'd like to stick with normal practices and procedure to the extent possible. Second, at trial we are going to need a testifier on this issue and that testifier can't be Joe. Needless to say, the assigned revenue agent should be someone well-regarded and in whom you have the highest degree of confidence.

Thanks again for your continued assistance. Let me know if you have any questions.

David

Joe, knowing these calculations would take a few days, got right on them. He worked long hours, ensuring that every number was correct, even triple checking his work. Given how much new evidence we'd uncovered, the tax liabilities had shifted slightly, but not by much. Hunter still appeared to owe the United States government a great deal of money, most of which he'd incurred by illegally attempting to avoid paying taxes. As Joe worked, often taking his laptop home and spreading documents all over the kitchen table, David's mother was declining fast. By mid-July, she'd been told she had only a couple of weeks left.

Joe tried to balance the demands of the office with what was going on at home, which was often difficult. Watching his mother-in-law, Mary, enter the last phases of her life made him think about what was important in his own life. It also made him think of his father, also battling cancer. Joe didn't know how long he had left. He hoped he could get through this rough patch at work quickly enough go down and spend some time with him. Joe was at the office when he learned that Mary was likely at the end and spent his last moments with her in the hospital working on more calculations on the Hunter Biden case. He took the next day off to help David with funeral arrangements.

At home, he had more time than usual to flip through the news. He saw that interest in his case wasn't dying down in the media. If anything, it was intensifying. He also noticed that it was only right-wing outlets—or outlets he considered "right wing" at the time—that seemed to care about bringing Hunter Biden to justice. In *The New York Times* and on CNN, there was little mention of the case. And when it *did* get mentioned, it was usually stories filled with sympathetic quotes from friends of the Biden family. By this point, Hunter had published his memoir, *Beautiful Things*, and done several long interviews in the media to tell his side of the story.

And his side of the story, as far as Joe could tell, was that he was a grieving (fifty-something-year-old) kid with addiction issues. Anyone who criticized him or pointed out that he'd broken the law many times was nothing more than a right-wing psycho who wanted to embarrass the Biden family for political reasons. Mentioning all the less savory aspects of his life—the prostitutes, the child he refused to acknowledge, or the fact that he'd made porn videos with his dead brother's wife and uploaded them to adult video sites—was seen as beyond the pale in all the publications Joe had read for most of his life. It wasn't the kind of treatment anyone else—certainly not anyone on the other side of the political aisle—would get. It was hard to imagine, for instance, MSNBC looking the other way if Donald Trump Jr. had written this in a memoir as Hunter had written in *Beautiful Things*:

> I stayed in one place until I tired of it, or until it tired of me, and then moved on, my merry band of crooks, creeps, and outcasts soon to follow. Availability drove

some of the moves; impulsiveness drove others. A sample itinerary: I left the Chateau Marmont the first time for an Airbnb in Malibu. When I couldn't reserve it for longer than a week, I returned to West Hollywood and the Jeremy Hotel. There were then stays at the Sunset Tower, Sixty Beverly Hills, and the Hollywood Roosevelt. Then another Airbnb in Malibu and an Airbnb in the Hollywood Hills. Then back to the Chateau. Then the NoMad downtown, the Standard on Sunset. A return to the Sixty, a return to Malibu . . .

An ant trail of dealers and their sidekicks rolled in and out, day and night. They pulled up in late-series Mercedes-Benzes, decked out in oversized Raiders or Lakers jerseys and flashing fake Rolexes. Their stripper girlfriends invited their girlfriends, who invited their boyfriends. They'd drink up the entire minibar, call room service for filet mignon and a bottle of Dom Pérignon. One of the women even ordered an additional filet for her purse-sized dog.

Joe had read the book for the first time the week it came out just to make sure there wasn't anything that would change his case. There wasn't. He'd also listened to a few interviews, during which Hunter Biden had claimed he was the victim of a witch hunt. Which, Joe supposed, made him one of the angry villagers with a burning torch.

But none of that changed the fact that he still had a job to do, and that job was to follow the facts to where they led. And where they led in the Hunter Biden case was a courtroom. It wasn't Joe's job to make sure Hunter went to prison, or even that he pled guilty to his crimes. It *was* his job to make sure that Hunter was treated like everyone else. It was his job to get the charges in front of a judge and a jury, who would review the evidence we'd been collecting for almost five years now and decide what to do about it. Maybe it's because the death of his mother-in-law had put him in a philosophical frame of mind, but during the summer of 2022, Joe thought often about how people choose to spend their lives on earth. Some do crack and make excuses for themselves, wandering around until they find the next person who's willing to give them a pass, while others show up to work and do their jobs, even when those jobs aren't glamorous. He decided he was going to be the second kind of person.

Back at the office, prosecutors were still going back and forth with the IRS about what to charge and where to charge it. David Weiss had also gotten another letter from Senators Grassley and Johnson, this one dated July 7, asking whether he'd discussed special counsel authority. He hadn't responded to this one or the first one.

On July 29, during a prosecution team call, Lesley Wolf had confirmed what we had suspected: everything depended on what DOJ Tax was willing to authorize. And even then, the goalposts kept moving. Weiss had reportedly said he wanted to charge Hunter for the 2014 and 2015 tax years by the end of September, but there was an asterisk on that deadline—one big enough to stall the case indefinitely. Wolf made it clear that if Hunter's legal team requested any delays, those would have to be taken into account. Which meant that the timeline wasn't just in Weiss's hands; it was in the hands of Hunter Biden's own lawyers. Weiss also told us that the reason he wanted to charge by September was to avoid pushing up against the midterm elections.

This seemed ridiculous to us. The general election had been one thing, given that Hunter's father was one of two main candidates in the race. But Joe Biden wasn't a candidate in the midterms. It seemed like just another excuse to push things further down the line. By early August, things took another turn. The DOJ Tax attorneys assigned to case had finally given their approval for discretion to move forward with charges—but only for the 2017 to 2019 tax years. This seemed to undermine what Attorney General Garland had been saying about Weiss's authority in the case. And charges for those tax years wouldn't even be handled in Delaware. The proper venue, we were told, was the Central District of California.

Meanwhile, behind the scenes, the IRS was pushing back hard on DOJ Tax's decision. Field Operations Director Michael Batdorf urged IRS leadership to make it clear that they still supported charging the 2014 and 2015 tax years. Without those charges, the case would be stripped of its most damning evidence. It would also allow Hunter's Burisma income to remain untaxed, effectively allowing him to avoid paying massive amounts to the government.

Things between prosecutors and Hunter's legal team were heating up. During a prosecution team call on August 12, one of the prosecutors let us know that during his last contact with Chris Clark, one of Hunter's lawyers, Clark had said that if they charged his client, they would be committing "career suicide." Days later, on August 16, we sat down with Weiss. It was during this meeting that we realized just how much had been kept from us.

Weiss, for his part, said he still agreed that Hunter should be charged for the 2014 and 2015 tax years—but that DOJ Tax had concerns. Their argument, the same one we'd heard before, was that a jury might be too sympathetic to Hunter Biden, given his past drug use and the death of his brother. As if juries hadn't convicted people with addiction issues before. As if grief excused criminal behavior.

Gary wasn't having it. He pointed out that ignoring the 2014 tax year meant erasing one of the clearest examples of wrongdoing—the unreported Burisma income, which would go untaxed. Without it, the picture of Hunter Biden's financial misconduct would be incomplete.

After the Weiss meeting, we reconvened with our FBI counterparts, who had come to the same conclusion we had: Delaware prosecutors had been keeping key details from us, and they weren't acting alone.

The next day, August 17, Gary sent an email to his supervisors summing up what we were all thinking:

> Venue . . . would be the [C]entral [D]istrict of California. This is new to us and shows their lack of transparency. My theory is that they never discussed that venue because it would have revealed what they were leaning towards, in terms of charging, months ago.

On August 18, IRS Field Operations Director Batdorf sent an email to his colleagues at the IRS letting them know he was pushing for a meeting with the DOJ Tax leadership, including Stuart Goldberg, to formally state the IRS's position: the 2014 and 2015 tax years needed to be charged. Meanwhile, DOJ Tax attorney Mark Daly sent an update outlining the tentative schedule ahead. It included approvals for three witness interviews in mid-September and a planned preview of the case before the U.S. Attorney's Office for the Central District of California the week of September 19.

On August 24, Gary got an email from FBI supervisor Garret Kerley, who let him know that Lesley Wolf had provided him with inaccurate information concerning a case update. This had resulted in incorrect information being sent up the chain. To fix it, Kerley emailed Wolf in an attempt to set up clearer lines of communication, copying several members of the team.

He wrote:

All,

I know we have our monthly meetings, but dissemination of information in between those meetings is being missed. At least for me, I am finding out about meetings, updates, and interviews well after the fact, which is causing me to send wrong information to my HQ. I figured with everyone's schedules, the easiest way to correct this is through an email chain or going back to weekly meetings.

My thoughts are to send this email out every Monday and everyone just reply if they have updates, meetings, etc. for the week. If you don't, then just reply "No."

If anyone has a better idea, please let me know. If not, I will send this first email out on Monday.

A/SSA Garret Kerley
Federal Bureau of Investigation
Baltimore Division / Wilmington RA
C-11

In response, Lesley Wolf told him to "stand down." And he did.

Around this time, prosecutors had settled on attempting to charge Hunter in the Central District of California. Although this wasn't where the investigation had been conducted, it was where he had committed many of the crimes. They supposedly could have brought charges at any time, but instead, they waited. In early September, President Biden appointed Martin Estrada, a former federal prosecutor, to become the U.S. attorney in that district. Rather than move forward immediately, prosecutors waited until Estrada was confirmed and sworn in on September 19.

That same day, thirty-three Senate Republicans sent a letter to Attorney General Merrick Garland, urging him to grant special counsel status to U.S. attorney David Weiss. Their letter stated:

> Given that the investigation involves the President's son, we believe it is important to provide U.S. Attorney Weiss with special counsel authorities and protections to allow him to investigate an appropriate scope of potentially criminal conduct, avoid the appearance of impropriety, and provide additional assurances to the American people that the Hunter Biden investigation is free from political influence.

Meanwhile, Weiss was attempting to present the case to the newly sworn in Martin Estrada, a Biden appointee who obviously should have recused himself. It was one of the first things on Estrada's calendar the week of September 19. Notably, the briefing that Weiss and Estrada had on that day did not include tax year 2014.

Once again, we requested to attend the meeting, and we were denied. The day after the briefing, Gary emailed Weiss for an update. He wanted to know whether we'd be able to bring charges in the Central District of California before the midterms.

By now, he should have known the answer was no.

During a call on September 22, Lesley Wolf told us to be patient. Estrada needed to "learn to be a U.S. attorney," and he wouldn't be able to read all our memos as quickly as we'd like him to. Given these circumstances, we weren't going to be able to bring charges before the midterms—doing so, according to Wolf, would be "shooting ourselves in the foot." So we had to wait again. And the hope that anything would ever come of all this waiting was rapidly diminishing.

After that meeting, Gary sent a few emails. One was to Mike Batdorf, which read: "Big news on Sportsman . . . Bad news. Continued inappropriate decisions affecting timing i.e. election. We can talk later if you are busy . . . I believe their actions are simply wrong and this is a huge risk to us right now." To Batdorf and a few other special agents at the IRS, he wrote: "During today's [Sportsman] team call there was some information provided to the team concerning decisions made by the USAO and DOJ that need to be discussed. For example, the AUSA stated that they made a decision not to charge until after the election. In itself, the statement is inappropriate let alone the actual action of delaying as a result of the election. There are other items that should also be discussed that are equally inappropriate."

On September 23, Gary met with FBI assistant special agent in charge Ryeshia Holley to discuss his concerns. Holley emailed everyone to set up a meeting with David Weiss and Jason Poole. Around the same time, Joe got a call from IRS special agent in charge Darrell Waldon—who knew very little about the case—indicating that DOJ Tax didn't expect to indict Hunter Biden until at least 2023 due to various levels of approval within DOJ Tax.

That same day, Joe traveled to New York City with Christine Puglisi to interview James Biden, who'd finally agreed to speak with him after many months of haggling over the terms of the interview. Joe was glad it was happening, although he was deeply frustrated that he was not allowed to question James directly about his dealings with Joe Biden. During this interview, James

Biden confirmed his close personal and business relationship with Hunter, describing himself as both a mentor and protector. He acknowledged that Hunter had struggled with addiction throughout their dealings and often failed to show up to meetings or left abruptly when he did show up. James recounted their involvement in business ventures, including an ill-fated hedge fund deal, and their connections with CEFC China Energy. James Biden downplayed his own role, claiming he had primarily been looking out for Hunter's interests, even as he acknowledged receiving payments through Hunter's company, Owasco. He also addressed Hunter's infamous diamond gift from a Chinese associate, claiming it turned out to be worthless. When asked about Hunter's financial dealings, he insisted he had little direct involvement but was aware that money had moved through intermediaries, including Rob Walker. Throughout the interview, he portrayed himself as someone who had tried to help his nephew navigate business while minimizing his own level of engagement in any questionable transactions.

This wasn't necessarily revelatory information, but it was all part of building the case. After a few days of moving back and forth—which had to be delayed further because Gary took a trip to the Netherlands—leadership finally decided on a meeting that was tentatively set for October 7. Gary would attend with Darrell Waldon, and several members of leadership at the FBI and DOJ would be there. In advance of the meeting, Gary emailed Ryeshia Holley at the FBI to ensure that his agenda items would be covered.

He wrote:

Ryeshia,

This is of course in Delaware, correct? I assumed but the invite did not specify.

Also, do you have a top three items you plan to raise so we can be on the same page?

My list includes the following as the top three items:

1 Special counsel
2 election deferral comment – continued delays
3 venue issue?

Of course these just scratch the surface of issues but I think it is best if we are united and to stick to the most important topics.

Thanks again.

Holley wrote back two days later to confirm that all three of these items would be discussed. Her email hit Gary's inbox around 4:30 p.m. on October 6, 2022. By this point, however, no one was interested in planning for the meeting.

They were all talking about *The Washington Post*.

That morning, a story had hit the internet.

The headline was:

FEDERAL AGENTS SEE CHARGEABLE TAX, GUN-PURCHASE CASE AGAINST HUNTER BIDEN
Delaware U.S. Attorney David Weiss, a Trump appointee, must decide whether to charge the son of the current president

At first glance, this didn't seem like a huge deal. We saw stories from time to time that analyzed the work we were doing. Our standard procedure was to skim them, look for key details, and flag them for discussion at our next prosecution meeting if we thought anything we'd read was worth mentioning.

Joe saw the article first. Right away, he realized he was dealing with something much different from an ordinary newspaper story, most of which were written by outsiders with no in-depth knowledge of the case. This reporter seemed to have details that weren't available to anyone in the general public.

"Federal agents investigating President Biden's son Hunter have gathered what they believe is sufficient evidence to charge him with tax crimes and a false statement related to a gun purchase," the reporter wrote, "according to people familiar with the case. The next step is for the U.S. Attorney in Delaware, a Trump administration holdover, to decide on whether to file such charges, these people said."

The phrase "people familiar with the case" was the one that caught Joe's eye. As he kept reading, it became clear that whoever the reporter's source was, that person had clearly worked on this case. There was a strong possibility, given how much this person knew about our interview schedule, that he or she could have worked in the very building Joe was sitting in as he read. And if that person's identity was ever revealed, it was unlikely that he or she would be working in the building much longer.

As several people at the IRS pointed out that day, the leaker stood a pretty good chance of going to prison.

Far down in the story, there was a long pair of quotes from Christopher Clark, the attorney Hunter Biden had hired largely to make the case go away. In a written statement sent directly to the reporter from the *Post*, Clark had said, "It is a federal felony for a federal agent to leak information about a Grand Jury investigation such as this one. Any agent you cite as a source in your article apparently has committed such a felony. We expect the Department of Justice will diligently investigate and prosecute such bad actors. As is proper and legally required, we believe the prosecutors in this case are diligently and thoroughly weighing not just evidence provided by agents, but also all the other witnesses in this case, including witnesses for the defense. That is the job of the prosecutors. They should not be pressured, rushed, or criticized for doing their job."

All day, rumors swirled about where the leaks might have come from. Some people put forth psychological profiles of the people they imagined might have leaked the material. By the end of the day, most people agreed that the leaker was (a) a frustrated investigator who felt shut out of the process, (b) someone who'd attempted to move the case forward with little success, and/or (c) a person prone to chatting and sharing details about his life to anyone who might be around Hunter Biden's defense team. It didn't take a police sketch artist to let us know what just about everyone at IRS and DOJ headquarters—certainly everyone who'd been involved with the Sportsman case—was thinking.

We were the leakers.

Before October 6, we thought we'd been in a tough situation. People at the office believed that we were difficult and that we had no faith in our superiors to let us do our jobs. But after October 7, we learned the true meaning of "tough situation." Now, in addition to merely thinking we were annoying, our superiors believed that we had potentially committed a violation of Rule 6(e) of the Federal Rules of Criminal Procedure, the federal statute that makes it a felony to leak grand jury information—one that is punishable by up to five years in prison.

For some people, this would have been a breaking point. The whole time we'd been discussing the need for a special counsel, we had also been discussing the possibility of blowing the whistle.

But we still weren't there. Gary figured he could keep it together for a little longer. He believed he would know his breaking point when he saw it.

Which he did, about twenty-four hours later.

EIGHT

RED LINE

"**CAN YOU BELIEVE** he said that?" Gary asked. "I mean, can you *believe* he said that?"

He was sitting behind the wheel of his government-issued sedan. On his lap were handwritten notes he'd taken during his meeting with David Weiss, his associates at the U.S. Attorney's Office, and about a dozen other people from the FBI, IRS, and DOJ. Special agent Darrell Waldon, who'd traveled to attend the meeting, peeked over from the passenger seat of the car to see what Gary was pointing at.

There, in the middle of the page, was the sentence: *Weiss stated that he is not the deciding person on whether charges are filed.*

Sitting there in the parking lot of the Delaware U.S. Attorney's Office, Gary could still remember the shock he'd felt at David Weiss saying these words in the meeting. For months now, Weiss had been assuring anyone who would listen that he had full autonomy to bring charges wherever he wished to bring them. Attorney General Merrick Garland had said the same thing under oath many times. If what Weiss had said during the meeting Gary and Darrell had just attended was true—and Weiss himself had assured everyone that it was—both of these men might have misled Congress. Easing himself back into the passenger seat, Darrell said, "Yeah, I know. I couldn't believe it."

He didn't sound nearly as surprised as Gary thought he should have. Just to drive the point home, Gary ran down the rest of his notes, giving an account of all the things that had surprised him during the meeting. Darrell agreed halfheartedly with most of it. By the time Gary dropped him off at the train station a few minutes later, they'd only covered about 10 percent of the shocking things that had just occurred.

As he drove back toward the D.C. area in complete silence—no radio, no podcasts, just the sound of the road under his tires and a slight ringing in his ears—Gary played back the other 90 percent in his mind. He remembered the way Weiss had looked shortly after he admitted that he had no power to charge Hunter Biden with crimes. He was sheepish, almost like he'd allowed himself to say too much. From there, he also admitted that he'd requested special counsel authority, and it became clear to Gary why he'd been so cagey about addressing this issue in public. Although Weiss never came out and said he'd been denied the special charging authority that would have come with a special counsel appointment, he was almost positive that this was the case.

There'd been other jarring items on the agenda, so many that Gary's hand had begun to cramp up as he tried to get it all down. But he had. Now he needed to decide what to do about it. Just before he dropped Darrell off at the train station, he'd told him he was going to write an email to upper management and cc him. This was important, given that Darrell had been the only other IRS rep in the room. Darrell had told him he'd look out for the email. Now, about three seconds after he'd pulled into his driveway, Gary was at his laptop furiously typing out his handwritten notes while the meeting was still fresh in his mind. When he was done, he reviewed it twice, then sent it to Mike Batdorf with Darrell copied.

It read:

Mike,

Darrell asked me to shoot an update from today's meeting. Darrell—feel free to comment if I miss something.

1. Discussion about the agent leak—requested the sphere stay as small as possible
   a. DOJ IG will be notified
   b. FBI HQ is notified and they refer it to their Counter Intelligence squad in a field office for investigation
   c. IRS-CI – **We need to make a referral to TIGTA** – What do you need from me on this action item?
2. **Weiss stated that he is not the deciding person on whether charges are filed**
   a. I believe this to be a huge problem—inconsistent with DOJ public position and Merrick Garland testimony
   b. Process for decision
      i. Needs DOJ Tax approval first—stated that DOJ Tax will give "discretion" (We explained what that means and why that is problematic)
      ii. No venue in Delaware has been known since at least June 2021
      iii. Went to D.C. USAO in early summer to request to charge there—Biden-appointed USA said they could not charge in his district
         1. USA Weiss requested Special Counsel authority when it was sent to D.C. and Main DOJ denied his request and told him to follow the process
      iv. Mid-September they sent the case to the

> Central District of California—coinciding with the confirmation of the new Biden-appointed USA—decision is still pending
>   v. If CA does not support charging, USA Weiss has no authority to charge in CA
>   1. He would have to request permission to bring charges in CA from the Deputy Attorney General/Attorney General (unclear on which he said)
>   vi. With DOJ Tax only giving "discretion" they are not bound to bring the charges in CA and this case could end up without any charges
> 3. They are not going to charge 2014/2015 tax years
>   a. I stated, for the record, that I did not concur with that decision and put on the record that IRS will have a lot of risk associated with this decision because there is still a large amount of unreported income in that year from Burisma that we have no mechanism to recover
>   b. Their reason not to charge it does not overcome the scheme and affirmative acts—in my opinion
> 4. FBI SAC asked the room if anyone thought the case had been politicized—we can discuss this if you prefer
> 5. No major investigative actions remain
> 6. Both us and the FBI brought up some general issues to include
>   a. Communication issues
>   b. Update issues
>   c. These issues were surprisingly contentious
>
> Always available to discuss. Have a great weekend!

After he hit Send, it occurred to Gary that "surprisingly contentious" didn't quite capture just how weird things had gotten in the room after he brought up the various delays in the case. When it became clear that Gary was suggesting the prosecutors were acting improperly, people grew defensive. Things got so awkward that you could practically feel it in the air. As the meeting broke up and people darted out of the room in different directions, most with solemn looks on their faces and their gazes cast downward, Gary knew something had shifted in the case.

Early in the morning after the three-day weekend, Darrell Waldon emailed Gary and Mike and said, "You covered it all." In other words, Waldon agreed with Gary's account of the meeting, and he'd admitted it in print. Batdorf thanked them both for their "continued communications." In the months to come, Waldon would claim that none of what Gary said in that email had actually happened, relying on lawyerly language to say that he "did not recall" what was actually said. He also stated that if he had taken notes, he would have thrown those notes away while cleaning his office. Gary never figured out why Waldon would claim this. But it didn't matter. They'd both been in the room that day, and they'd both heard David Weiss say what he said.

Back at the office, Joe felt he was being threatened with prison for the first time, based on the statements from Chris Clark in *The Washington Post* article.

Obviously, someone could potentially believe that he was one of the individuals who'd leaked details of the investigation to the *Post*. This didn't scare him much, mostly because he knew he'd done nothing wrong. But it was unsettling nonetheless.

Once his last interview was over, Joe had very little left to do but wait and bother people for updates in the case. During a prosecution team meeting on October 17, we were told that there was not a grand jury to issue subpoenas out of. When we asked when Martin Estrada, the Biden-appointed U.S. attorney in California, might make a decision about whether he wanted to partner with David Weiss and bring charges, Mark Daly said,

"I'm not the boss of them." A few weeks later, Weiss told Darrell Waldon that he would no longer be speaking with Gary. A few days after that, Lesley Wolf reached out to Joe to ask for all of the reports and emails Gary had written related to the Hunter Biden case.

This was a strange step. Joe was used to being asked for things like this for discovery purposes. But this seemed to be something else. DOJ seemed to want to review everything Gary had done regarding the case, which was not something you did if you weren't looking for reasons to remove someone from an investigation. Right away, Gary knew that whatever excuse they were ultimately given, it would be a ruse. By now, DOJ must have realized that Gary was a diligent note-taker who often sent emails with critical comments about the way prosecutors were handling the investigation. They clearly wanted to comb through his emails for anything that might make them look bad.

Around this time, there were plenty of other people working to make management at the DOJ look bad. One of them was Hunter Biden's attorney Christopher Clark. On October 31, 2022, Clark wrote a thirty-one-page letter to David Weiss that blasted the investigative team for leaks and other untoward actions. The letter also contained threats, which seemed to be commonplace in the Biden camp. Among other things, Clark said that if the investigation moved forward, President Biden would need to take the stand as a witness. He said that this was only necessary because of the leak of information that had occurred on October 6—a leak he blamed on someone close to the investigation.

"President Biden," he wrote, "now unquestionably would be a fact witness for the defense in any criminal trial . . . This of all cases justifies neither the spectacle of a sitting President testifying at a criminal trial nor the potential for a resulting Constitutional crisis."

This seemed to have the effect that Clark and the Biden camp intended. Prosecutors were chilled. From that point on, we heard almost nothing from the team. Around that time, the statute of limitations for the 2014 tax charges expired—despite Hunter's attorneys previously signing waivers to extend them. The prosecution team meeting that we were supposed to have the following day was abruptly canceled.

Something was going on. And no one was telling us what it was.

Wanting to stay in the loop and keep things moving, Gary emailed Lesley Wolf to say that the next meeting—whenever it happened—would be important to get things back on track. He proposed a few dates in December, but he never heard back. At the same time, he knew, prosecutors were busy combing through his emails and reports trying to figure out how much of what Gary had documented might come back to bite them later on.

The answer, we knew, was *a lot*.

But at this point, we were still trying to move the case forward, knowing all the while that it was probably impossible. On November 9, Gary emailed FBI assistant special agent in charge Ryeshia Holley, writing, "Since our discussion on October 7 where we, again, discussed the lack of communication/transparency from their office it appears they have doubled down and we have received almost nothing since then. With the canceling of today's pros team meeting and recent unusual requests for discovery it is important to ensure we have an open line of communication with them." The next day, he emailed David Weiss with dates that the IRS and FBI were available to meet again. But we never got anything back. From this point on, the higher-ups at the Department of Justice handled the case alone, shoving away any input from the agents at the IRS and FBI who'd made the case.

In a matter of days, we were shut out from the rest of the team. Although we didn't know it at the time, Weiss and the rest of the team at the DOJ were finding ways to go around us. In early December, we learned from Mark Daly that IRS special agent in charge Darrell Waldon would be the main point of contact at the IRS for the case from now on. On December 13, the staff of the Delaware U.S. Attorney's Office and the Department of Justice had a meeting in Delaware that lasted all day. We only heard about it when it was over.

Presumably, the meeting centered on our fight to bring the case in California. We'd been struggling with this for some time, and Martin Estrada still hadn't gotten back to us about whether he was willing to partner with the Delaware U.S. Attorney's Office to bring charges. Given everything we knew about Estrada—starting with the fact that he'd been appointed by Joe Biden—this didn't seem likely. Ever since Hunter Biden's lawyers went on the offensive in October, a chill had come over the case. No one wanted to touch it for fear that they'd be retaliated against—or, of course, that they would spark a "constitutional crisis" by attempting to charge the president's son with crimes that he had, in fact, committed.

It's worth mentioning that this kind of talk began only when Joe Biden took office. All throughout the first Trump presidency, members of the president's family were pursued aggressively by law enforcement officials, most notably at the FBI. No one, to our knowledge, ever suggested going easier on him because he was the president. If anything, the opposite was true.

In late 2022 and early 2023, we heard rumors that Martin Estrada was not going to take the case in California. This meant that for the time being, it wasn't going to be charged anywhere. After years of hard work, threats, and an unprecedented four taxpayer conferences with Hunter Biden's attorneys, the case was effectively dead.

That same January, Chris Clark met with David Weiss in Delaware. During this meeting, Clark told Weiss that his legacy would be defined by how he handled the decision on whether to charge Hunter Biden. Shortly thereafter, Gary learned that case meetings were being held without our knowledge. Weiss seemed to have shut out the IRS completely. When he learned that there had been a meeting between prosecutors and the FBI on January 19, he wrote an email to Mike Batdorf and Darrell Waldon, his only remaining links to the case within the IRS.

The conversation went as follows:

Shapley to Batdorf and Waldon—January 20, 2023, 10:58 a.m.

Mike/Darrell,

I am a little confused as to what the current expectations of me are and would like to ask for clarification. Delaware has stopped communicating with us and excluded investigators because of a leak—or at least that's what they said. But now they've brought back the investigators from the FBI, just not the IRS. I'm trying to manage this investigation while being completely shut out.

I've been the primary point of contact on this case since January 2020, meeting with DOJ Tax, U.S. Attorneys, and others, and that hasn't changed under SAC Waldon. But now I don't even know what's expected of me. Please let me know how you'd like me to proceed.

Waldon to Shapley—January 20, 2023, 11:01 a.m.

They brought the investigators back from the FBI? Did the FBI tell you this?

Shapley to Waldon—January 20, 2023, 11:05 a.m.

Yes sir, that's my understanding too. The meeting yesterday was with FBI leadership and investigators. Joe got a readout from FBI case agent Mike Dzielak.

A side note: the third FBI case agent/SSA in charge of this case is retiring this week. He wasn't mandatory, but it's another shift in the team.

Waldon to Shapley—January 20, 2023, 11:18 a.m.

Gary,

It's my understanding, based on my discussion with David, that investigators on the Sportsman case have not been brought back. The FBI asked about the case, but they were given the same update I was: they're wrapping up their process. No substantive decisions have been made, though more meetings with attorneys—including defense—are coming up.

Regarding additional targets, Jason Poole should reach out next week. It sounds like Tax will be handling those.

I relayed this to Joe this morning via conference call. That's all for now.

Things continued in this strange manner for a few months. We could tell we were off the case, but we didn't have official confirmation of it yet. Meanwhile, Hunter Biden's attorneys—specifically Chris Clark, who'd been on the warpath for a long time—were continuing to intimidate and shake down anyone they felt might eventually help bring their client to justice. In February, Clark wrote a letter to Michael Horowitz, the inspector general at the Department of Justice, regarding an investigation into the leak of grand jury materials that occurred in October 2022. We knew that many people at the DOJ suspected we had something to do with this leak, which we did not. Clark also reached out to many officials at the DOJ asking whom he could appeal to if David Weiss did decide to charge Hunter Biden. In the end, he emailed associate deputy attorney general Brad Weinsheimer.

All the while, we were aware that David Weiss had no authority to bring charges. He'd said so himself (no matter what everyone else who'd been present while he said it would later report). But this didn't stop Attorney General Merrick Garland from stating the opposite in public, even while he was under oath. In response to a hearing question from Senator Chuck Grassley on March 1, Garland said, "The United States Attorney has been advised he has full authority to make those referrals you're talking about or to bring cases in other districts if he needs to do that. He has been advised that he should get anything he needs . . . I have not heard anything from that office that suggests they are not able to do anything that the U.S. Attorney wants them to do."

Gary had seen enough of these interviews by now to know that they were going to keep up the act. Every time an official from the federal government—which, again, was controlled by Joe Biden and his appointees—had to testify under oath about the Sportsman case (although the public didn't yet know it was called that), they would use the same short phrase, repeating it like a magic spell to deflect all criticism. That phrase was

Trump-appointed U.S. attorney. If someone suggested that Joe Biden or one of his associates might be attempting to tip the scales in favor of his son, they'd point out that David Weiss, who'd been appointed by Donald Trump, was in charge. Once during congressional testimony, FBI Director Christopher Wray didn't even bother using Weiss's name. He just said a "Trump-appointed U.S. attorney" was in charge.

But Weiss wasn't in charge.

We knew it, and so did every person who'd been at that meeting on October 7, 2022. In the months to come, as he went back and forth on whether to come forward and say something, Gary would come to think of the single hour he spent in Delaware as his "red line meeting." Before it, he was willing to believe that all the misconduct he'd witnessed had been accidental, or at the very least not malicious. After it, everything became clear. These misstatements about Weiss's authority were no accident.

It was time to do something.

All throughout the fall of 2022, Gary had been thinking about blowing the whistle. Things had gotten so bad at the office that it was beginning to affect his personal life. He wasn't sleeping. He was drifting off during dinner and thinking about his work, wondering how to move forward with his career given the way we'd been sidelined from the investigation. He knew what was happening was wrong, but he also understood that taking action could come at a tremendous personal cost.

We spoke about it often. Every time the subject came up, Joe would beg Gary not to do it. He was terrified that if Gary came forward and blew the whistle on all we'd seen, it would lead to

Joe being officially removed from the case. And without Joe on the case, we were all but certain that the case was going to be buried forever. Everyone on the team would be just fine either lying about it or pretending they didn't remember all the things we'd seen. There was no internal debate among the higher-ups, no confusion about what was going on—just a widespread, unspoken agreement to look the other way.

For months, well into the winter of 2023, Gary kept at bay the impulse to come forward. But the sleepless nights grew longer. Sometimes he'd find himself in front of his computer at three o'clock in the morning scrolling through dense legal texts, reading and rereading the statutes that governed whistleblowing, tax privacy, and grand jury secrecy. He emailed himself notes on the precise practices for handling protected information.

The statutes were long, and they were difficult to understand, even for someone whose job it was to parse the dense, bureaucratic language of the IRS. The more he read, the more he realized that whistleblowing wasn't just a matter of telling the truth—it was about navigating a legal minefield without stepping in the wrong place. He couldn't just walk into the office of a U.S. attorney and tell them what had happened. If he disclosed certain details improperly, he wouldn't just lose his job—he could face criminal charges. So he researched more. He documented everything—every meeting, every deviation from standard procedure, every time prosecutors delayed, ignored, or pushed aside evidence. He wasn't just collecting evidence; he was building a case for himself, making sure that if the time ever came, he would be ready.

Somewhere in the back of his mind, he probably always knew that he was going to have to blow the whistle. But he couldn't bring himself to admit it. He always felt there was more research to conduct, more planning to do. He sometimes hoped that he'd find a disclosure rule that would make it impossible for him to come forward, leaving the task to someone else.

But all he found were rules. Rules that protected the guilty. Rules that made it nearly impossible for the people investigating corruption to actually expose it. Rules that, for months, had kept him awake at night.

The more he read, the more tangled the process became. There was no simple way to do this—no open-door policy that would allow him to report what he had seen without consequence. The laws governing tax investigations were written in a way that made it nearly impossible to share information without risking criminal penalties. Every statute seemed designed to keep people like him silent.

Two laws in particular governed his every move: 26 U.S.C. § 6103, which restricted the disclosure of tax return information, and Rule 6(e) of the Federal Rules of Criminal Procedure, which mandated secrecy around grand jury proceedings. These weren't just bureaucratic hurdles, they were federal statutes carrying severe penalties, including prison time. Even if he wanted to come forward, it could only legally be done to the House Ways and Means Committee, the Senate Finance Committee, or the Joint Committee on Taxation. Those were the only channels explicitly allowed under Section 6103. Anything else—leaking documents, talking to the press, even disclosing the existence of the investigation to unauthorized officials—could have meant the end of his career and, possibly, his freedom.

The language of Section 6103 was dense, but the intent was clear:

Returns and return information shall be confidential, and except as authorized by this title . . . no officer or employee of the United States . . . shall disclose any return or return information obtained by him in any manner. (26 U.S.C. § 6103(a))

This wasn't just about keeping a taxpayer's identity private. The statute defined "return information" broadly—it covered everything from income and deductions to payments, liabilities, and audits. Even referencing details from an ongoing tax investigation could be a violation. The law treated tax data as if it were classified intelligence—and in many ways, it was.

He was also bound by grand jury secrecy laws, specifically Rule 6(e), which dictated that nearly everything discussed in a grand jury setting had to remain sealed. It was designed to protect the integrity of an investigation, to keep witnesses from being intimidated, and to prevent leaks that could compromise a case. The rule was just as ironclad as Section 6103:

Unless these rules provide otherwise, the following persons must not disclose a matter occurring before the grand jury: (i) a grand juror; (ii) an interpreter; (iii) a court reporter; (iv) an operator of a recording device; (v) a person who transcribes recorded testimony; (vi) an attorney for the government..." (Fed. R. Crim. P. 6(e)(2)(B))

There were limited exceptions. Prosecutors could discuss grand jury matters within the government as long as it was necessary for their work. Certain disclosures were permitted by court order. But there was no easy path for a whistleblower who wanted to reveal missteps he'd seen at the highest levels of his organization.

For weeks, Gary wrestled with the implications of these laws. If he made even a minor misstep, he could become the story. The people who had shut down the case could turn around and prosecute him for mishandling protected information. He had seen it happen before—when the government wanted to silence someone, it didn't take much to find a reason. His safest option was legal representation, but that came with its own complications. Most whistleblower attorneys focused on financial fraud, environmental violations, or government waste. Few had experience dealing with the unique mix of tax law, grand jury secrecy, and federal whistleblower protections that governed this case.

At first, he consulted a whistleblower attorney who, by most accounts, leaned to the left politically. The idea was to hedge against accusations of partisanship—to make it clear that his decision to come forward had nothing to do with politics and everything to do with the integrity of the law. But after several months, it became obvious that their priorities didn't align. The attorney didn't fully understand Section 6103, wasn't experienced with Rule 6(e), and—perhaps most troublingly—seemed hesitant to take the case forward at all.

As he worked with this attorney, who'd come at the recommendation of a friend, Gary began to suspect he was trying to "catch and kill" the Hunter Biden story. He hadn't felt this way at the beginning. But as soon as the lawyer—who, as mentioned, leaned to the left—started to suspect the case Gary intended to blow the whistle on was against Joe Biden's son, he began to exhibit the same stonewalling tactics Gary was trying to blow the whistle on in the first place.

Everywhere Gary turned, more walls went up.

Finally, after he parted ways with that first lawyer, Gary remembered a talented attorney he'd worked with on a previous case. Mark Lytle had been working at the U.S. Attorney's Office in the Eastern District of Virginia back then. He and Gary had prosecuted Credit Suisse for tax-related conspiracy, resulting in $2.6 billion from Credit Suisse. Since then, Mark had gone into private practice.

Mark was the Chief of the Financial Crimes and Public Corruption Section at the Office of the U.S. Attorney for the Eastern District of Virginia.

Gary knew that if there was anyone on earth who understood the tax secrecy statutes, it was Mark. Gary reached out in December 2022, and Mark agreed to take the case pro bono—even before he knew who the subject was. Mark knew that if Gary needed help, Mark would not turn him away. This time, when Mark got the idea it might be Hunter Biden, he wasn't intimidated and didn't bat an eyelash. He just kept charging ahead, researching and laying out exactly how Gary needed to go about legally blowing the whistle.

Mark noted that it was dangerous. It would come with bad press, and it would probably come with even more sleepless nights than Gary was already experiencing. At this point, Gary was certain he did not want to do this. If there were any other way to handle it, he would have taken it. But there wasn't. It was either come forward or let the stress consume him. Over a period of months, Mark and Gary worked to find the right people who could help them bring this to Congress—which, according to the law, was the only appropriate venue for whistleblowers to air such sensitive complaints.

That search led them to Tristan Leavitt and Jason Foster, two attorneys who specialized in whistleblower protections and had deep knowledge of how Congress handled sensitive disclosures. Their nonprofit Empower Oversight was established to provide pro bono legal assistance to whistleblowers, and they agreed to help with Gary's case. Tristan had just departed a term on the three-person Merit Systems Protection Board that decided federal whistleblower cases, where he'd been nominated by President Biden and confirmed by the U.S. Senate. Understanding the relevant whistleblower protections and how they intersected with Congress, Empower Oversight also began researching the taxpayer privacy laws.

That was when they hit the most bizarre legal roadblock of all—one that most people, even experienced attorneys, wouldn't have seen coming.

Gary was extremely limited legally by the law in what he could tell even his own attorneys about the case. This was because of 26 U.S.C. § 6103, the federal statute that guarded tax return information with the same secrecy as classified intelligence. Under this law, not even Gary's own lawyers could hear the details of what he knew until Congress explicitly authorized them to do so.

It was an insane reality: here was a man risking everything to come forward, convincing a team of attorneys to specifically help him navigate the legal maze—and the law itself barred him from even telling them what was going on.

The law was clear, and there was no gray area.

> Returns and return information shall be confidential, and except as authorized by this title . . . no officer or employee of the United States . . . shall disclose any return or return information obtained by him in any manner. (26 U.S.C. § 6103(a))

But there was one exception.

According to 26 U.S.C. § 6103(f)(4)(A), three congressional committees had the authority to receive confidential tax return information. But for other specific individuals—such as legal counsel—to review it, they had to be designated by one of those committees. That meant that before Gary could say a word to his attorneys about Hunter Biden, Burisma, tax return details, or anything else, Congress had to formally grant his attorneys the authority to hear it. Until that happened, his own legal team was working in the dark.

This forced them into a strange, almost absurd waiting period. Gary and his legal team—which, for all intents and purposes, was the best of the best—could talk about the process, like which committees they would approach and how, what steps would come next. However, he couldn't tell them a single name, a single number, a single specific detail. It was like preparing to testify in court while not being allowed to say what the case was about. Still, Gary and his attorneys spent hours going over the laws and procedures together for coming forward.

There was at least one thing his legal team recommended prior to going to Congress. His lawyers helped connect him with staff for the inspector general at the Department of Justice. Given his past working for the inspector general at the NSA, he knew how important this step was. But even his lawyers couldn't actually sit in as he made all of his protected disclosures to the Office of Inspector General.

Still, even being able to share with the inspector general's staff felt liberating. Finally he could unload all the details of what he'd seen over the past several years.

And with a legal team helping him navigate the legal landmines, he also now had a process. A path forward.

For the first time in a long time, he was moving toward something instead of trying to ignore it. And for the first time in months, he was sleeping again.

Because now, rather than being complicit in something he knew was wrong, he was finally trying to fix it. Rather than being stuck on the inside of a corrupt machine, he was taking steps outside.

Still, he was well aware that he had a man stuck on the inside.

And in the first months of 2023, with accusations of leaking and other criminal violations flying all over the place, that man was not happy.

He was freaking out.

PART THREE

WHISTLEBLOWERS

NINE

BLOWING THE WHISTLE

LATE IN 2022, a right-wing Twitter account called Marco Polo posted a picture of Joe in a rainbow tutu.

The photo was real. It had been taken in June 2019 during an event for Gay Pride. David, his partner, was right beside him in the photo. In the tweet, the photo sat against a mass of black text that purported to be a "dossier" about the IRS's handling of the Hunter Biden case. It looked like something a lunatic had put together in his basement. Which, by the way, it was. And the lunatic in question's name happened to be Garrett Ziegler (no relation). Ziegler's dossier, several screenshots of which were posted to his "Marco Polo" Twitter account, contained other pictures of Joe. Two of them showed him in Speedos on the beach; another, shockingly, was an image of his driver's license with his home address on it.

The text of the tweet read:

> @MarcoPolo501c3: The lead IRS agent responsible for investigating the Bidens is on the left— in the tutu.
> More info on the agent and his "partner" . . . on pages 74-75 in our dossier.

The tweet contained a link to David's Twitter account. Several people piled on in the comments, mocking Joe for being gay and intimating that he was almost definitely going to take it easy on the Bidens. They wondered how a gay Democrat could possibly be objective enough to charge Hunter Biden with tax crimes.

The irony was enough to make Joe want to scream. Scrolling through these disgusting, hate-filled tweets in early January 2023, he'd felt like throwing his phone against the wall. At the very least, he wanted to tell all these weird losers that *he* was one of the only people at the IRS who *did* want to bring charges forward. But he managed to avoid this temptation. Saying anything would only make it worse.

The tweets had come to Joe's attention just after Christmas of 2022 when an FBI agent called him from a blocked number to let him know they were out there. This agent also let Joe know that the bureau had picked up credible threats against him and his family. He wanted to know if Joe needed someone to come out to the house and sit with him just to make sure no one stopped by and tried to kill him.

"I'm fine," he said. "But I'll let you know if I change my mind."

For right now, all he cared about was getting the case across the finish line.

All throughout the first months of 2023, when it was clear there wasn't even a finish line in sight, Joe maintained hope. Whenever he heard that there had been some development in the case, he'd reach out and ask about it. Sometimes he'd offer to help; other times he'd just ask to be kept informed about what was going on.

Almost no one answered him.

Gary was still coming to the office every day, going about his business as usual. His days were full. He was still performing his usual duties at the office, overseeing cases and working with the agents under him to keep those cases moving forward. But he was even more diligent now about keeping records and taking notes. And now, when he was done with those notes, he didn't just file them away. He'd review them for hours, preparing for the moment when it was finally time to come forward.

We never spoke in the office about blowing the whistle. That happened after hours, usually during long FaceTime calls. Some nights, Gary would warn Joe that he might eventually have to testify about the case as well. As Joe's supervisor, Gary was careful not to pressure Joe into blowing this whistle unless Joe wanted to. But it was a big step, and Joe wasn't ready yet. In part, this was due to a difference in our temperaments. As a case agent, Joe believed that as long as he was still technically on the case, he could keep charging ahead and somehow bring things to a close. But every development he heard about told him that this wasn't likely.

On March 16, for instance, Mark Daly was overheard speaking to Jack Morgan, a fellow DOJ Tax attorney, saying DOJ Tax would give David Weiss the approvals he needed to charge the tax stuff if he wanted to, but that he had no idea where Weiss planned to charge Hunter Biden. Two U.S. attorneys, both appointed by Hunter Biden's father, had declined to take the case without giving a reason. We couldn't bring the case in Washington, D.C., where we first went to for the earlier tax years, and we couldn't bring it in California, where Hunter Biden had lived when he filed the fraudulent returns. For the moment, we were stuck. No one knew what to do.

On April 13, after hearing that Hunter Biden's lawyers were going to meet with the Department of Justice at the end of the month, Joe emailed Lola Watson, his assistant special agent in charge in IRS-CI. All throughout his time at the IRS, Joe and Lola had gotten along well. He figured she was his best shot at figuring out where he stood. Trying to keep a friendly, optimistic tone, he wrote:

> Hi Lola –
>
> So I wanted to put some stuff in front of you regarding updates I am hearing on the Sportsman Et Al investigation, that I am not hearing through you or Kareem, which is concerning to me. I don't think that you or Kareem have any reason to keep things from me, but I wanted to make you both aware of some of these updates.
>
> So I have heard that Sportsman's counsel is meeting with Main DOJ at the end of this month—I would consider this a significant update.
>
> I had heard that Sportsman's counsel met with David Weiss in February—I have not heard any update from the result of that meeting.
>
> I have heard that David is currently asking for the Pros Memo from DOJ-Tax approving the tax charges—I would consider this a significant update indicating that David is seeking authority to charge. This was right after Merrick Garland's testimony.
>
> The last we heard about this Pros Memo from DOJ-Tax was in August of 2022, in that it was moving to John Cain's 3rd party review.
>
> Regarding the ▊▊▊▊▊ investigation I have heard that there is a draft of an email search warrant that we are not being included in. The case and information related to ▊▊▊▊▊ and information obtained via our tax

BLOWING THE WHISTLE

investigation. It seems as if we are now being completely removed from this investigation whereas we used to work as a team with the FBI. The results of an email search warrant matter because ████████ and Sportsman, and if in those emails, there is indication that it is not, that would have potential tax implications on Sportsman and ████████ —This is a risk area to us and why I believe we need to continue our involvement in this investigation. We need to figure out how to fix this issue, so that we can become a team once again with the FBI in Delaware. If our agency doesn't want us involved in this investigation, please let me know and I will back off.

The ████████ and ████████ investigations are continuing to move along, but our tax investigation of ████████ has completely stopped since September of 2022—With no idea of how we are going to work this investigation and get it to completion.

There are updates happening, and we aren't being notified in one way or another and it appears like there is still a breakdown in communication—If this relates to the leak investigation, I need to know that as well.

Please let me know if you have any further questions.

A few minutes after hitting the Send button, Joe received a phone call from Lola's boss, special agent in charge Kareem Carter. Kareem was curt and accusatory on the phone with Joe, telling him that they were being as transparent as possible and they were not hiding any information from the team, but Joe knew that this wasn't true. Still, for some reason, he held out hope. This was a complicated case, and it was unlike anything he'd ever worked before. Just because he was being shut out for the moment didn't mean he'd be shut out forever. Gary, who was a little ahead of Joe in his thinking, was no longer holding out hope at all. Again, he let Joe know that whenever he was ready to blow the whistle, Gary would be there to help.

But Joe had his own red line, and it was a little further away than Gary's. All along, as we'd spoken in hushed tones about blowing the whistle, Joe had known that if he was ever removed from the case outright—as in formally removed, with a phone call or an email telling him so directly—he would have no choice but to come forward. What he couldn't have known, of course, was that the IRS had agreed in December 2022 to remove us both, months before even Gary came forward and blew the whistle.

By mid-April Gary and his legal team were ready to pull the trigger on going to Congress. The legal team had prepared a letter to various congressional committees identifying the fact that a confidential IRS employee wanted to make protected whistleblower disclosures to Congress, but needed one of the relevant committees to authorize his attorneys to receive the confidential taxpayer information so they could help him prepare his disclosures. Since both Jason Foster and Tristan Leavitt had worked as staff for Republicans in Congress, including "the godfather of whistleblowers," Senator Chuck Grassley, they decided it would be better if the initial letter was signed only by Mark Lytle. The text of the letter would undoubtedly leak to news organizations, and they didn't want any issue—even imagined ones of attorney bias—to detract from the important facts of the letter itself.

Gary reviewed the draft of the letter to Congress many times. Once it was sent, Gary knew there was no going back. This whole thing would blow wide open, and it would make the dust-up about the leaks to *The Washington Post* that had occurred last

October seem small by comparison. In the span of an hour, he read the letter maybe twenty times, making sure every word was in its right place. Even after all he'd gone through, the sound of the words still had the power to shock him:

> Dear Chairs and Ranking Members,
>
> I represent a career IRS Criminal Supervisory Special Agent who has been overseeing the ongoing and sensitive investigation of a high-profile, controversial subject since early 2020 and would like to make protected whistleblower disclosures to Congress. Despite serious risks of retaliation, my client is offering to provide you with information necessary to exercise your constitutional oversight function and wishes to make the disclosures in a non-partisan manner to the leadership of the relevant committees on both sides of the political aisle.
>
> My client has already made legally protected disclosures internally at the IRS, through counsel to the U.S. Treasury Inspector General for Tax Administration, and to the Department of Justice, Office of Inspector General. The protected disclosures: (1) contradict sworn testimony to Congress by a senior political appointee, (2) involve failure to mitigate clear conflicts of interest in the ultimate disposition of the case, and (3) detail examples of preferential treatment and politics improperly infecting decisions and protocols that would normally be followed by career law enforcement professionals in similar circumstances if the subject were not politically connected.
>
> Some of the protected disclosures contain information that is restricted by statute from unauthorized disclosure to protect taxpayer and tax return information.

My client would like to share the same legally protected disclosures with Congress—pursuant to 26 U.S.C. § 6103(f)(5) and the protections afforded by 5 U.S.C. 2302(b)(8)(C)—that he has already shared with other oversight authorities. Out of an abundance of caution regarding taxpayer privacy laws, my client has refrained from sharing certain information even with me in the course of seeking legal advice. Thus, it is challenging for me to make fully informed judgments about how best to proceed.

My goal is to ensure that my client can properly share his lawfully protected disclosures with congressional committees. Thus, I respectfully request that your committees work with me to facilitate sharing this information with Congress legally and with the fully informed advice of counsel. With the appropriate legal protections and in the appropriate setting, I would be happy to meet with you and provide a more detailed proffer of the testimony my client could provide to Congress.

Sincerely,
Mark D. Lytle
Partner

But every word of it was true. And once that letter went out, Gary knew it would be his job to prove it to the world. Because he knew the attacks were coming.

This was the moment he had been dreading for months—the moment when all of the forces that had tried to bury the case would turn their attention on him.

On April 19, when Mark Lytle sent the letter to various congressional committees, Joe was trying to keep busy with other cases. He didn't even read the full text of the letter. But he couldn't miss the threatening statement to the press from Christopher Clark, Hunter Biden's lead attorney, about the whistleblower letter. Outlets like *The New York Times* trumpeted around the country Clark's allegation that "[i]t appears this I.R.S. agent has committed a crime."

Even worse was what Clark was writing behind the scenes. Shortly after Mark's letter went to Congress, Clark sent a private letter to the Department of Justice and the Delaware U.S. Attorney's Office—the first of many angry letters he would write about us. Despite the fact that Lytle's letter made no reference to Hunter Biden, or even the jurisdiction where the case was being investigated, Clark accused the IRS agent behind Mark Lytle's letter of disclosing both confidential taxpayer information *and* grand jury material. If Joe had seen this letter, he probably would have had to take breaks to stop his hands from shaking.

All along, Gary had assured Joe that he was working with some of the best lawyers in the world. He said he'd gone over the laws governing whistleblower disclosures so many times that he could practically recite them by heart. So he felt the threats Clark was making were nothing more than empty bluster, the kind of thing hard-charging lawyers do for their clients so they feel like they've earned the hundreds of thousands of dollars in legal fees.

But Joe didn't know any of that for sure.

For all he knew, the government might decide to ignore the letter of the whistleblower statutes and throw Gary in prison for illegally disclosing information anyway. It certainly wouldn't have surprised him, given all that we'd learned over the past five years about the way decisions get made at the highest levels of government.

This early flurry of activity was a warning about what would happen to Joe if he ever did decide to come forward. Suddenly, he would become the subject of a very public fight involving some of the most reviled political figures in the world. His social media accounts would be fair game. So would every email he'd ever sent to his colleagues at the IRS. He didn't feel ready for that kind of scrutiny. Not to mention the fact that coming forward and testifying against the people you worked with—people whom, for the past five years, you'd grown extremely close with, sharing intimate details about your life and listening to stories about their lives—could make things extremely awkward at the office. And that was assuming he didn't just get fired immediately after blowing the whistle.

It was a lot to think about.

Late that month, before anyone knew Gary was the secret whistleblower who was about to tell Congress everything, we both watched as Danny Werfel, the IRS commissioner, testified before the House Ways and Means Committee. We didn't know Commissioner Werfel. As a general rule, staffers at the IRS kept the commissioner insulated from most of the work we did. Anything Werfel heard about was something he might later be called to testify about in front of Congress, so he tried to hear as little as possible.

Toward the beginning of the hearing, Commissioner Werfel was asked by Chairman Jason Smith of Missouri whether he'd commit "that there will be no retaliation against the whistleblower." Commissioner Werfel came back quickly with a canned answer: "Mr. Chairman, while I can't comment on a specific case, I can say without hesitation there will be no retaliation for anyone making an allegation or a call to a whistleblower hotline."

After the way the past week seemed to be going for Gary, he was happy to hear the commissioner say this. But it didn't give him much comfort. After all, he knew better than anyone that public officials could lie under oath.

In fact, they seemed to do it all the time.

On April 24, Mark Lytle was contacted by associate deputy attorney general Bradley Weinsheimer, who worked high in the Justice Department bureaucracy. Weinsheimer requested a phone call, which they arranged for the next day. In it, Weinsheimer said that the Department of Justice would "love" to speak with Gary.

But the very next day, Weinsheimer and Weiss had a meeting with Christopher Clark about the Hunter Biden case. When we later learned about this, it seemed clear to us that DOJ's offer to speak with Gary was not about hearing his side—it was about gathering intelligence. They wanted to know what he knew so they could prepare for whatever Gary was about to say, and we wouldn't have been surprised if they'd been willing to pass that information on to Hunter's legal team as well—all in the name of "fairness," of course.

Finally, in late April both the House Ways and Means Committee and the Senate Finance Committee sent letters to Gary's attorneys Mark Lytle and Tristan Leavitt officially designating them as cleared to hear Section 6103-protected information. Only then could Gary actually tell them the details of what he was coming forward with.

With that obstacle cleared, they met together in Mark's Nixon Peabody offices near Washington, D.C.'s Chinatown to finally read-in Mark and Tristan. Over two full days, they made Gary tell his story again and again and again—so many times that he would get sick of hearing himself talk.

They also began preparing the evidence, assessing what records he had, how best to organize them, and which ones were necessary. And as an investigator, Gary took that part seriously.

He wasn't about to walk into Congress and make accusations without proof. He had over 120 documents that he knew were critical to showing the extent of what had happened. But given his Hill experience, Tristan tried to temper Gary's expectations about what kind of evidence would be most useful to Congress. Given the Ways and Means Committee's past release of President Trump's tax returns, there was a significant chance these committees would also consider voting to release whatever materials Gary provided. But that would require each committee member reading the materials, and dumping hundreds (maybe thousands) of interview transcripts, email chains, and contemporaneous notes onto the desks of members of Congress was not likely to endear him to the committees. "They're not going to want all of that," Tristan said. And it would likely delay the committees' consideration of the materials. He suggested starting small and giving a broad picture, while making clear they were prepared to provide more documents about any of the topics Congress might request. But Gary insisted that he be thorough.

"I don't care what they want," Gary shot back. "If I'm going to go up there and accuse my bosses of lying, and of obstructing this investigation on purpose, I'm not going to end the sentence with, 'And that's my opinion, guys.' I want facts." He knew that many people—especially lawyers for Hunter Biden—were going to come at him and say he was exaggerating, or that he'd made the whole thing up. The proof needed to be ironclad.

He wasn't a political operative, and he wasn't here to play by Washington's unspoken rules. His job was to present the evidence, not to worry about how much Congress did or didn't feel like reviewing it. He wasn't going to stick his neck out and make these accusations only to have people dismiss them as unsupported claims. He needed the evidence to speak for itself.

In the end, they compromised.

On May 5, Mark and Tristan had a proffer session with staffers at the House Ways and Means Committee, followed by a second proffer session with staffers at the Senate Finance Committee. Proffer sessions are preliminary meetings where a witness, usually through their attorney, provides information to investigators under the understanding that the statements won't be used against them in future legal proceedings unless they are later found to be false. They're used to assess the credibility and value of a witness's testimony before granting formal protections or proceeding with an investigation. Mark and Tristan reported back to Gary that the proffer sessions went well, and it appeared the committees would next want to interview Gary directly.

On May 15, assistant U.S. attorney Lesley Wolf wrote to Hunter Biden attorney Christopher Clark, offering a deferred prosecution agreement for Hunter Biden that required no guilty plea whatsoever. Clark accepted and even offered to draft the language himself.

We didn't know any of this at the time. And as far as Gary could tell, things on the whistleblower front were moving along as planned. But inside the office, things were worse than ever. We were still shut out of meetings on the Sportsman case. No one was getting back to us. There were rumors that Hunter Biden would soon be offered an extremely favorable plea deal, but we couldn't confirm them. By mid-May, we were hoping—wishing—that someone would just say something, even if it was a stern reprimand or an email officially removing us from the case.

And on May 15—the same day Christopher Clark was being offered a sweetheart deal by the Department of Justice—we got our answer.

That afternoon, on a phone call with special agent in charge Kareem Carter, with assistant special agent in charge Lola Watson also on the line, we were officially removed from the case. The Department of Justice, we were told, had requested a brand new team of agents. None of the twelve special agents under Gary's supervision would be allowed anywhere near it again.

This was retaliation—clear and unmistakable retaliation—for the protected disclosures Gary and Joe made to their leadership in the IRS and DOJ throughout the investigation and for Gary's decision to come forward. It was exactly what IRS Commissioner Werfel had sworn under oath would not happen. Gary was furious. But he wasn't surprised. All throughout the process, he'd been preparing for something like this to happen. He just didn't think it would be so blatant.

Joe, on the other hand, wasn't angry at all—not yet, at least. He was devastated.

―

After the call, he cried.

Then he cried again.

For almost a year now, he'd known he wasn't going to be on the case much longer. But that didn't make it any less painful when he actually heard the words.

By now, the case had very little to do with Hunter Biden or the dozens of people Joe had interviewed for it. It was about something much bigger. For the past five years, he'd been doing everything he was supposed to do, working for an organization to which he had given most of his adult life. He'd gone above and beyond to bring the case forward, traveling on weekends and spending long hours every night making sure everything was in perfect shape. He'd made good friends while working this case, even if they did occasionally clash.

And now he was finding out that it was all probably going to come to nothing.

Like most people, Joe had constantly questioned himself about the potential of just letting go of the case.

Because I can't, he always wanted to say to himself. *Working cases is my job, and I'm not going to stop doing my job just because the people above me don't like what's going to happen if I keep pushing forward.*

To his partner David, more often than not, he said nothing. Sometimes he mentioned the possibility of blowing the whistle, always speaking in generalities to avoid disclosing information that David wasn't allowed to know. David usually said this sounded like more trouble than it was worth. He'd been deeply affected by the abuse the two of them had endured on social media, and he didn't want more of it.

The juice, in other words, *wouldn't be worth the squeeze.*

Still, there was no denying that Joe's red line had been crossed. He'd been saying for months that if leadership decided to remove him from the case, he'd have no choice but to blow the whistle. This had sounded like a good plan in theory, especially back when he couldn't imagine leadership ever doing something like that. But now it had happened, and it was time to step up. He called Gary for the number of a good attorney, and Gary connected him with another Empower Oversight colleague, whistleblower expert and former Grassley staffer Dean Zerbe.

After a brief phone call, Joe decided he was ready to come forward. He learned that he didn't need to reveal his identity the way Gary planned to reveal his. There were ways to testify without becoming a public figure, which was Joe's greatest fear all along. The small taste of fame he'd gotten when his identity had leaked was more than enough for him. He wanted the world to know what he knew, but he didn't necessarily want the world to know anything about him. In his mind, he wasn't the story. The story involved everyone above him who'd failed to act the right way at every step of the Sportsman investigation. At the end of the phone call, Joe told Dean to let him know what the next steps were.

For the next two days, he walked around in a daze. He spoke with Gary often, trying to get more assurances that he wasn't going to break the law by coming forward.

Then, on May 18, he got the urge to write an email.

It started small at first, just notes on what he'd been going through. Then it became a theoretical exercise—just a few quick words about what he *might* say to Commissioner Werfel and all his other superiors if he ever got the chance. Even as he watched the email on his screen grow to include many paragraphs, he didn't think he'd send it.

But after about an hour of walking around the office and thinking about it, he decided to throw some names in the "To:" field and type out a subject line. The names were his entire chain of command from the commissioner on down: Daniel Werfel, Douglas O'Donnell, James Lee, Guy Ficco, Michael Batdorf, Kareem Carter, and Lola Watson. The subject line was "Sportsman Investigation - Removal of Case Agent."

Then he sent it.

Just before ten o'clock in the morning on Thursday, May 18, all the people mentioned here received the following message:

My Respective IRS Leadership –

First off, I apologize for breaking the managerial chain of command, but the reason I am doing this is because I don't think my concerns and/or words are being relayed to your respective offices. I am requesting that you consider some of the issues at hand.

As I am sure you were aware, I was removed this week from a highly sensitive case out of the USAO after nearly five years of work. I was not afforded the opportunity of a phone call directly from my SAC or ASAC, even though this had been my investigation since the start.

I can't continue to explain how disappointed I am by the actions taken on behalf of our agency. I want to echo that I love my job, I love my agency, and I am extremely appreciative of the job and position that I have had over the last 13 years.

There is a human impact to the decisions being made that no one in the government seems to care about or understand. I had opened this investigation in 2018, have spent thousands of hours on the case, worked to complete 95% of the investigation, have sacrificed sleep, vacations, gray hairs, etc. My husband and I (identifying myself as the case agent) were publicly outed and ridiculed on social media due to our sexual orientation, and to ultimately be removed for always trying to do the right thing is unacceptable in my opinion. Again, my leadership above my direct manager—who was also removed—didn't even give me the common courtesy of a phone call, did not afford me the opportunity to understand why this decision was made, and did not afford me an opportunity to explain my case.

If this is how our leadership expects our leaders to lead, without considering the human component, that is just unacceptable, and you should be ashamed of yourselves.

For the last couple of years, my SSA and I have tried to gain the attention of our senior leadership about certain issues prevalent regarding the investigation. I have asked for countless meetings with our chief and deputy chief, often to be left out on an island and not heard from. The lack of IRS-CI senior leadership involvement in this investigation is deeply troubling and unacceptable. Rather than recognizing the need to ensure close engagement and full support of the investigatory team in this extraordinarily sensitive case, the response too often has been that we were isolated—even when I said on multiple occasions that I wasn't being heard and that I thought I wasn't able to perform my job adequately because of the actions of the USAO and DOJ. My concerns were ignored by senior leadership.

The ultimate decision to remove the investigatory team from ▬▬▬▬ without actually talking with that investigatory team, in my opinion, was a **decision made not to side with the investigators, but to side with the U.S. Attorney's Office and the Department of Justice, who we have been saying for some time has been acting inappropriately.**

I appreciate your time and courtesy in reviewing this email. Again, I can only reiterate my love for my work at CI and a great appreciation for my colleagues—and a strong desire for CI to learn from and be strengthened by my difficult experience. I never thought in my career that I would have to write an email like this, but here I am. Thank you again for your consideration.

Joseph Ziegler
Special Agent
International Tax & Financial Crimes Group (ITFC)
Washington DC Field Office

For the rest of the day, he heard nothing.

Then, in the following days, he heard from assistant special agent in charge Lola Watson.

Joe cringed as he opened the email, noticing that something was off from the very first line.

"Good afternoon Special Agent Ziegler," it read.

Special Agent Ziegler? Joe thought. In all the time he'd known Lola, she'd never called him anything other than "Joe."

Clearly, someone else had written this. The rest of the message only confirmed it.

> We acknowledge your email received yesterday morning. You have been told several times that you need to follow your chain of command. IRS-CI maintains a chain of command for numerous reasons, including trying to stop unauthorized disclosures. Your email yesterday may have included potential grand jury (aka 6e material) in the subject line and contents of the email, and you included recipients that are not on the 6e list.
>
> In the future, please follow previously stated directives and this written directive that no information should be sent to the DFO, Deputy Chief, Chief, or any other executive without being sent through my office and the SAC office.

For one thing, Lola had never mentioned anything to Joe about following the chain of command. So the first sentence was a lie. But on paper, it looked like Joe had disobeyed direct orders—which, it seemed, was what whoever wrote this email wanted anyone who read it in the future to believe.

But that wasn't the line that caught Joe's eye.

The thing that really made his heart race was the part about potentially including grand jury information in the subject line. He was sure he hadn't done this. There'd been nothing in the subject line of the email other than the code name of the case, which Joe knew was not 6(e) grand jury material. But he was also sure that leaking this kind of material was yet another crime punishable by some serious prison time. For the second time in just a few months, he'd been accused of serious wrongdoing simply for trying to move his case forward.

If he'd been on the fence about coming forward as a whistleblower before, he wasn't anymore.

It was time to come forward.

One weekend in late May as Gary prepared for his interview with the House Ways and Means Committee, he noticed someone outside his home surveilling it. It happened again the next day. He suspected someone had disclosed his identity to the press, which meant he could be outed any day. Rather than allowing others to define him when that happened, he decided to disclose his identity himself by taping an interview with Jim Axelrod at CBS News. He couldn't say much during this interview, but gave a broad account of what he'd seen as the supervisor on the investigation. "When I took control of this particular investigation," he said, "I immediately saw that it was way outside the norm of what I had experienced in the past." He was careful not to disclose the name of the investigation, the subject of the investigation, or even the district where the investigation was being conducted. Nevertheless, in between clips of Gary speaking, Axelrod shared over B-roll footage of Gary that CBS had independently learned from other sources that Hunter Biden was the subject of the case. But when Gary was asked about the subject of the investigation, he specifically said that he could not "confirm or deny" who it was due to tax secrecy laws.

This interview aired on May 24. Two days later, Gary sat for his transcribed interview with the House Ways and Means Committee. This didn't happen in public, which allowed him to get deep in the weeds. Over a period of many hours, Gary produced exhibits, discussed email chains, and laid out the case for the lawmakers in the room. He read a long opening statement that his lawyers had helped him prepare, making sure to note that although this case would probably help Republicans, he wasn't doing it for political reasons. The questions from staff for the committee were probing. Gary had to take frequent breaks. But by the end, he'd told almost all of the story, and he was happy with how things had gone.

Joe was up next. On June 1, he traveled to Washington, D.C., on his own dime and sat across from the same long wooden table that Gary had, telling his side of the story. Unlike Gary, who'd had a great deal of time to prepare and figure out what he was going to say, Joe was flying by the seat of his pants. As he spoke, he found himself putting things together that he hadn't even thought about before. He rambled in places, but for the most part, he thought he'd painted a good picture for the committee. After many hours, he was done.

At that point matters were in the committee's hands. Committee staff indicated the members of Congress on the committee would likely want to vote to release the transcripts of our interviews. But they couldn't be sure until they'd provided the transcripts to their members, along with all the evidence we'd shared as exhibits. Either way, our part was done. We'd made our disclosures to Congress, and now they could do with it what they would. We assumed there might be some follow-up questions or other work we might need to do to help them in their investigation, but now it was just a waiting game. Gary went out of the country in June.

It was the calm before the storm.

From the moment the Delaware U.S. Attorney's Office had learned we would essentially be deposed by Congress, they'd been very busy.

While we were working to put together the best testimony possible to prove that the Justice Department had done everything they could to protect Hunter Biden, those same officials had been working around the clock to craft a plea deal to (you guessed it) protect Hunter Biden.

After Christopher Clark volunteered to Lesley Wolf to draft the language of a prosecution deferral in May 2023, he'd gone looking for a template he could use. He found one in the 2011 Delaware USAO agreement with Aegis Electronic Group and emailed it to Wolf on May 19, 2023.

Initially, it seemed like they were closing in on a deal that would allow Hunter Biden to avoid jail time without entering a guilty plea. But then, on May 23, 2023, U.S. attorney David Weiss intervened, demanding that Hunter at least plead guilty to two misdemeanor tax charges. Undoubtedly knowing that our testimony to Congress would accuse him of mishandling the case in order to protect Hunter Biden, Weiss would have looked terrible if he ended up agreeing to a deal that allowed Hunter to skirt all the tax charges. Clark, furious, accused Wolf of misleading him and rejected the deal outright. Yet despite his objections, when he consulted Hunter Biden in his garage in Malibu, Hunter was still willing to take it.

On June 2, 2023, Clark made it clear in an email to Wolf that protection from future prosecution was a nonnegotiable condition of any deal. This was no longer just about Hunter avoiding a trial—it was about ensuring that no future administration could revisit the case.

Here's where things got unusual. Rather than placing all the key provisions into a single, integrated plea agreement—something that would undergo full judicial scrutiny—the government split the deal into two parts: a standard plea agreement for two misdemeanor tax charges and a separate diversion agreement related to a felony gun charge. And instead of including the government's broad promise of immunity—its agreement not to pursue other potential charges against Hunter—in the plea agreement, where the judge would be required to approve or reject it, prosecutors placed that immunity provision solely within the diversion agreement. Diversion agreements are typically used for low-level offenses and are handled outside the courtroom. They are supervised by the Department of Justice, not the judge, meaning the judge has no real authority to accept, reject, or even interpret their terms.

In practice, this meant that the most consequential aspect of the deal—the government's assurance that Hunter would not face future charges for a wide range of conduct—was effectively shielded from judicial review. Legal experts later pointed out that this arrangement was highly irregular. Normally, a grant of immunity like that would be subject to Rule 11 of the Federal Rule of Criminal Procedure, which governs plea agreements and requires a judge to ensure that the deal is fair, voluntary, and lawful. By embedding it in the diversion agreement instead, prosecutors created a kind of legal gray zone—raising serious questions about whether they were intentionally sidelining the court.

Either way, as the Delaware U.S. Attorney's Office negotiated with Hunter Biden's legal team, they knew they were in a race against time. The Justice Department had just a few weeks to finalize the deal before the House Ways and Means Committee likely made our allegations public. DOJ needed to shut the door on any future charges before we could expose exactly how they'd slow-walked the case and obstructed key investigative steps.

By the third week of June 2023, the House Ways and Means Committee was ready to schedule an executive committee meeting to vote on releasing our transcripts. But on June 20—just as committee staff were preparing to issue a public notice of the meeting—they were blindsided when the Justice Department formally announced Hunter Biden's plea deal, filing two documents in the District of Delaware. DOJ *had* beat the shot clock.

To those of us familiar with the case, the terms of the agreement were shocking in their leniency. The plea agreement was a sweetheart deal that would enable him to wriggle free of the most serious charges. What's more, the announcement seemed to communicate to the public that there wasn't really much of a case against Hunter Biden. In an interview on MSNBC, Christopher Clark was highly complimentary to the Delaware U.S. Attorney's Office, saying the prosecutors there were "very diligent, very dogged. It took five years, and it was five years of work they put in." When the interviewer responded: "Five years ... [And] what they came up with was two misdemeanor tax counts," Clark must have had a hard time keeping glee off his face as he replied carefully, "That's the resolution we have."

The public was in for some whiplash when two days later, on June 22, the House Ways and Means Committee voted to release the transcripts of our testimonies publicly, as well as supplemental affidavits we'd provided with more evidence. Gary's name would be right at the top of his testimony, whereas Joe's name would be redacted. In the press, he'd be known as "Whistleblower X," a name his lawyers had decided on.

The news reports came immediately. Every day, Gary and his legal team got new media inquiries from people who wanted to know what had really happened with the Hunter Biden case—and what would happen next.

Given that we were no longer on the case, we weren't receiving any further information on the latter question. But all we knew was that the American public seemed very interested in what we had to say. So interested, in fact, that the House Committee on Oversight and Accountability asked us immediately whether we would be willing to testify publicly, right there in the Rayburn House Office Building in front of hundreds of thousands of people watching from home on television.

For Joe, that would mean casting the pseudonym aside— losing the anonymity that protected him from the sort of abuse he'd previously received when he was outed on Twitter. For a while, he wrestled with the decision. But he knew all along that he'd say yes. Even as he was telling David, who still insisted he was supportive, that he wasn't sure what to do, he knew on some level that he was going to have to step forward eventually.

As he weighed the decision, he thought back to a moment he'd had with his father a few years earlier. They were sitting together in the his father's house. Joe had come to spend some time with him. For some reason, Joe broached the subject of how brutal it had been for him to grow up as a closeted gay kid with a father who cracked jokes constantly about how devastating it would be for him to have a gay son. With his voice cracking, Joe told his dad that he'd always felt like he had to hide who he really was. For thirty years—throughout his childhood, his adolescence, and his first failed marriage to a woman—he'd walked around with a deep fear of revealing too much about himself, believing that if he said the wrong thing or acted the wrong way, his dad would be ashamed of him.

"I didn't know," his dad said, now crying. "I never wanted to make you feel that way."

"Well, you did," Joe said.

His father spent the rest of the night apologizing. It was the most cathartic moment Joe could remember having since he'd come out as gay a few years earlier at the age of thirty. Since then, his father had been immensely supportive. Now, as he moved inexorably toward the moment when he'd have to get in front of Congress and tell his story to the world, he felt a similar push and pull within himself. There was no doubt that he was afraid of what people would say. The torrent of hate that had come at him a few months ago when that Twitter account leaked his identity had done some serious damage to his self-esteem. And that had just been a few freaks on the internet. Now he would be a target of hate from millions of people all over the country, many of whom were invested in the Hunter Biden saga to an unhealthy degree.

At the same time, though, he knew it was the right thing to do. He knew that if he tried to hide now, someone would figure out who he was eventually—and they'd probably find out on their terms, not Joe's. It was better that he control the narrative and show the world what he'd uncovered. If the Department of Justice wasn't going to let Joe present his case, then he would do it himself. And Gary would be right beside him even if IRS leadership wasn't.

All throughout the process, David had said that he was supportive of Joe's decision to come forward. But Joe could tell he had a hesitation in his voice. Something about being outed publicly at the end of 2022 had spooked him. But there was more. A distance was growing between them, and Joe didn't know what it was. He figured there'd be plenty of time to investigate that (and to fix it) when he got through this ordeal with the Sportsman case.

Joe made the final decision to testify that summer. Almost as soon as he did, he began seeing headlines and cable news chyrons about his case everywhere he went, all asking the same question in bold type.

Who is Whistleblower X?

In July, he was going to give them an answer.

TEN

COMING OUT

"GOOD MORNING, BABE—You're going to kill it today."

The text message jolted Joe out of a sound sleep. When he opened his eyes, he saw the off-white ceiling of a hotel room. It took a few seconds for him to shake himself awake and remember that he wasn't home in Atlanta.

He was in a hotel room in Washington, D.C., about a mile from the Capitol building.

And he was there alone.

David had decided to go on vacation in Portugal for a few weeks, mostly so he wouldn't be home at the moment Joe's identity was revealed. As Joe got out of bed and stepped into the shower, he tried not to think about the fact that his marriage was on the rocks. He also wondered, as he had so many times over the past few months, whether the decision to come and testify had been the right one. There was no denying that it *felt* right. But there were plenty of arguments he could make against it.

For one thing, there were a lot of crazy people in the world. One of them might decide that Joe's testimony made him or her angry and come to his house to kill him. That was an extreme example, of course, but it wasn't like similar things hadn't happened in the past. Just a few years earlier, Joe had been robbed at gunpoint right in front of his house. At the end of 2022, some psychos on the internet had posted an image of his driver's license along with a bunch of other identifying information.

In other words, he had good reason to be a little skittish.

By the time he was out of the shower and preparing to dress, though, he'd perked up a little. He'd spent about eight hours the previous day with his lawyers preparing for every eventuality. They'd practiced his opening statement many times over, tweaking words and adding sentences until everyone was happy with it. Dean Zerbe, his lawyer, had arranged for some experts to come in and consult. One of these experts was a former commissioner at the IRS; others were former congressional aides who told him exactly what to expect once he got in front of the committee.

One thing they stressed was that not everyone would be friendly. Joe said he knew this. But they stressed that he *really* had to keep it in mind. Some members of Congress, they reminded him, were going to ask questions that were designed to make Joe say something stupid in public. Others were going to use the time to grandstand. One former aide said, "Some of these people just love to hear themselves talk. It's not a bad thing to let them run out their five-minute clock. When someone is really on a tear, don't interrupt them. And you don't have to provide an answer. Just let them go."

Joe filed this advice away along with everything else he'd been told over the past few days. After a few hours in the room, a friend of Dean's came in and let Joe know that his social media accounts were "clean." Joe asked what he meant, and one of Dean's associates let him know that he and a small team had been working for the past few days to review every post Joe had ever made on his social media, looking for things that lawmakers might bring up during the testimony. As Mike spoke, Joe thought of all the shirtless selfies and Speedo pics he'd posted over the years, cringing as he imagined what some of those photos might look like blown up on posterboard behind members of Congress.

But those weren't the kind of posts they were talking about. Mostly, they'd looked to see whether Joe had posted anything overtly political—anything that investigators might use to prove that he was going after Hunter Biden to help Donald Trump and the Republicans. On this score, they said they'd found absolutely nothing. Joe could have saved them a lot of time and money, of course, and told them that there would be nothing. Even during the most intense years of the investigation, he hadn't been a particularly political person. He was a registered Democrat, just like all his friends. But he'd never been evangelical about it. Even more, he made the decision not to vote for president in the 2020 election in order to stay apolitical—and with the fear in the back of his mind that he may have to testify about it at a criminal trial.

Brushing his teeth, Joe thought about how strange it felt to be on the other side of an investigation. Rather than looking into other people, he was the one being looked into. His own lawyers were using the same techniques Joe had used over the years to investigate Hunter Biden and other tax cheats. It didn't feel great, but it was made slightly better by the fact that he knew he didn't do anything wrong. This hotel room—which he'd paid for out of his own pocket, along with the flight to D.C.—wasn't covered with crack cocaine and hookers the way Hunter Biden's hotel rooms had been. In fact, there was nothing in the room but a suitcase, some files, and a dark suit that had some serious miles on it by now.

Joe had worn the suit while interviewing James Biden a few months earlier. He'd worn it during the ill-fated "day of action" in December 2020. Now he was going to wear it in front of millions of people as he told the story of how the Sportsman investigation had gone completely off the rails. Before he left, he stuck the paper copy of his opening statement in his backpack and took one last long look in the mirror.

He removed the IRS-CI lapel pin that he'd worn almost every day for the past decade and placed it on the desk.

Then he donned an American flag lapel pin.

The last thing Joe did before the night of his hearing was open up Outlook on his government-issued computer and draft a quick email to his boss Gary Shapley, who was going to sit beside him and testify that next day.

It read, "July 19 Hearing Invite," and Joe attached the document he received from the House Oversight Committee inviting him to testify in front of Congress. Joe knew that Gary would send this up his leadership chain to inform them of their intent to publicly testify the following day.

That next day, Gary was sitting in the offices of the members of Congress, nervously running over his own opening statement in his mind. With few exceptions, he'd gotten the same treatment as Joe the day before. It was easier for Gary's attorneys to go through his social media because he didn't have any. As he intended to point out in a few hours, he had voted for candidates of both parties over the years. He had no political agenda to advance.

His testimony this afternoon would be about the truth, the whole truth, and nothing but the truth.

All morning, he'd been watching Republican members of Congress stream through the room. They all shook his hand and thanked him for being there. It was strange to see all these people whose speeches and hearings he'd been following for years up close. For the first time, he considered what a stressful job this must be: every day, you got up in front of millions of people and spoke, knowing that any single wrong word could get you in enough trouble to end your career. Preparing to do this for just one day, Gary had felt like he was going to have a heart attack.

But now, with only a few hours to go before he was set to testify, he felt strangely calm. All he had to do was tell people what happened, ignore leading questions, and tell the truth as he saw it. He'd already turned over plenty of documents to bolster his assertions, and he had a team of lawyers to stop him from saying anything he wasn't legally allowed to say. For the time being, the threats from Hunter Biden's legal team and the worries about all the public scrutiny he was about to face were far from his mind.

And if he got stuck, he could always throw a question to Joe, who, at that moment, was . . .

. . . speeding toward the dome of the United States Capitol building on a Lime scooter, not far from the spot where he'd met Gary for the first time just a few years earlier. He found it hard not to think about that first meeting, which had occurred after meeting with their colleagues at the IRS. Back then, the thought that we would someday be near the Capitol dome testifying in front of Congress would have seemed unlikely, to say the least. At the start of the Hunter Biden investigation, we'd been two faceless employees of the IRS. No one cared what we had to say. Now, we had a story that millions of people wanted to hear. Thinking about this, as well as everything else he'd been through over the past few years, made Joe cry like a baby as he sped through town. Anyone who saw him must have thought he was out of his mind.

Finally, he pulled himself together and parked the scooter. It was around ten o'clock in the morning. Beside the rack was a group of photographers and reporters. A few hours from now, they'd crowd around Joe to take pictures. For now, though, they had no idea who he was. All of these people presumably knew that Whistleblower X would soon be testifying; what they didn't know was who that person was or what he looked like. Joe walked right past the photographers on the way in, trying to enjoy the last moment of anonymity he'd ever have.

Inside the Rayburn House Building, he found a few more reporters. They didn't know who he was either. He proceeded down the hall, wandering around alone until he came upon a door labeled "chairman." There, he found Gary and a few members of the committee. Beside them was a large door that led to the hearing room, where the show would begin around one o'clock. On the television, that same question was blaring: *Who is Whistleblower X?* The sound wasn't on, but Joe could read the lips of Harris Faulkner as she reported the story for her viewers at home.

We spoke with a few members of the committee's staff. They were all unfailingly polite and grateful that we'd come to share our story. They asked if we had any questions, and we said no. Our lawyers had prepared us for just about everything. Before we knew it, we were being marched into the hearing room, hearing the large wooden doors creak open as the cameras flashed and the members of the committee took their seats.

Chairman James Comer kicked things off with a few procedural things, then said, "This is an important joint effort to show people that accountability matters regardless of your last name." He then went over the progress that the House Committee on Oversight and Accountability had made collecting evidence against Hunter Biden and his family, much of which had come directly from us. As he spoke, we thought about how incredible it was that things had gotten to this point. While we were sitting in front of Congress making protected whistleblower disclosures, our leadership was somewhere else. No one other than our lawyers came with us that afternoon to testify.

It didn't have to be this way. The leaders of agencies should stand by whistleblowers working for those agencies. Nothing stopped members of our team or our colleagues at the FBI and the DOJ from showing up and supporting us. Just because we were alleging that their bosses had committed serious breaches of ethics didn't mean that they had to turn their backs on us.

But that's exactly what they did.

When Joe spoke, he spoke without the support of anyone at the IRS other than Gary. After Comer introduced him, Joe said:

> Honorable members of Congress, guests, and fellow citizens, today I stand before you, not as a hero or a victim, but as a whistleblower compelled to disclose the truth. With a heavy heart, I come here determined to accurately share my testimony in the hope that justice may prevail and the trust in our democratic institutions can be restored.
>
> I have come forward to this committee at your invitation—just as I previously came forward to the House Ways and Means Committee at their invitation. On June 1, 2023, I testified before the House Ways and Means Committee as an anonymous whistleblower (Whistleblower X), and I am here before you today, testifying in public as Joe Ziegler, a thirteen-year special agent with the Internal Revenue Service, Criminal Investigation Division. I believe that I have a duty to bring the public—and their elected representatives—full transparency of the facts as I know them regarding the criminal investigation of Robert Hunter Biden.

We live in a society built upon the pillars of transparency, accountability, and the rule of law. Importantly, no one person is above the law. These pillars are meant to ensure that power is used in the interest of the people and not for personal gain or hidden agendas. Yet, it is with great regret that I reveal to you the shadow that looms over our federal legal system.

I have witnessed the corrosion of ethical standards and the abuse of power that threaten our nation. It is within this context that I have chosen to shed light on these actions and expose those responsible. I recognize that while I was present at the start of this investigation and was closely involved with it for roughly five years, I'm just a part of the story. Others—including my colleague and supervisor Gary Shapley, who is here with me today—have their own views and understandings of what took place during this investigation.

Whistleblowers play a vital role in our society, shining a light on the darkest corners and risking personal reprisal for the greater good. Let me emphasize that my testimony is not an attack on any specific individual or political party. My aim is to address systemic problems that have allowed misconduct to flourish. It is not a call for blame, but a call for accountability and reform. At the end of the day, these are ultimately the two reasons for me being a whistleblower. I believe that we need to hold those accountable for their unethical and inappropriate behavior so that we can learn from our mistakes, create policy, and implement reform to ensure this doesn't happen again in the future.

Transparency is the foundation of our democracy. Without it, people lose their trust in institutions, and the bonds that tie the fabric of our nation begin to fray. The American people deserve to know the truth, no matter how uncomfortable or inconvenient it may be for either political party or those in power.

I had recently heard an elected official say that I must be more credible because I am a gay Democrat married to a man. I'm no more credible than this man sitting next to me due to my sexual orientation or my political beliefs. I was raised to always strive to do what is right. I have heard from some that I am a traitor to the Democratic Party and that I am causing more division in our society. I implore you, if you were put in my position with the facts as I have stated them, that you would do the exact same thing—regardless of your political party affiliation.

I hope that I am an example to other LGBTQ people out there who are questioning whether to do the right thing at a potential cost to themselves and others. We should *always* do the right thing, no matter how painful the process might be. I kind of equate this to coming out—it was honestly one of the hardest things I ever had to do. I contemplated scenarios that would have been highly regrettable. But I did what was right, and I am sitting in front of you here today.

I would like to take a minute to thank some people for their unfettered help and support. First off, God—for giving me the strength and courage to go through this process. My husband, who has been my rock, has put up with me and my stress and has had to deal with his personal information being displayed on social media as a part of this matter. My attorney, Dean Zerbe, who has agreed to represent me pro bono and has provided so much help and guidance through this process. The investigative team—the work that was done on this case is tremendous but seems to have been overshadowed by what is happening here today. I just want to say to the investigative team that I am thankful for having worked with you. My family and friends back home in Northeast Ohio and Georgia.

I do not live in the Washington, D.C., area. I have to fly here and have had to pay out of pocket for all of my travel-related expenditures in dealing with being a whistleblower. On that note, I would like to make the statement that I have not accepted a single payment from anyone for being a whistleblower.

And on he went, detailing the various missteps in the case that you've been reading about since page one of this book. His full testimony ran to about ten pages, single-spaced. Gary, who went next, filled in even more of the gritty details, telling the story in a way that was clear to anyone tuning in from home. He described all the ways that the case was hampered early on, as well as his consequential red line meeting with David Weiss.

Near the end, he turned his attention to the threats we'd been getting from Hunter Biden's legal team:

Even before Mr. Weiss told senior FBI and IRS leaders that he was not the deciding person on whether charges would be filed, Biden family attorneys attacked investigators in the pages of *The Washington Post* and threatened the prosecutors with "career suicide" if they brought charges against the president's son.

After my testimony was released, we received a request for a comment from a reporter claiming that Mr. Biden's attorneys had sent a letter to the Justice Department lobbying for a retaliatory criminal inquiry against me for my protected whistleblowing. The press did not share a copy of the alleged letter with us, and I still have not seen it. But, it is chilling to think that after threatening prosecutors with "career suicide," Mr. Biden's attorneys would be so bold as to actually lobby in writing for his father's Justice Department to prosecute the whistleblower who disclosed preferential treatment for the president's son.

Then one of the Biden family attorneys sent to the press a ten-page, error-filled letter addressed to Chairman Smith of the House Ways and Means Committee. It attacked me with innuendo, false statements, and baseless speculation that I had leaked information to *The Washington Post*. As I said in my affidavit to the House Ways and Means Committee, I did not leak information to any media source.

I sent *The Washington Post* a letter waiving any confidentiality of any communications I might have had with any of their reporters. So they could simply report that I was not the source. To the contrary, if I was the source, they could now report that I was the source and release the evidence, if they had any. But they have not and cannot because I told the truth in my affidavit to the House Ways and Means Committee.

Since both *The Washington Post* and I know I did not leak any information, they should not report on false attacks by the Biden family attorneys against me without correcting the record. All the paper will say is that it will not comment on sourcing. The American people should understand: this is an example of how you are being manipulated by false information.

I knew that coming forward to share the truth about an investigation into the president's son would not be easy. I stood to gain nothing, other than to satisfy my conscience. Making the decision to come forward once allowed me to sleep better, but being slandered and targeted by the government and the Biden family attorneys certainly has not.

I call on those senior leaders and agents at IRS-CI who know what is happening now to stand up for what they know is right because I need your support—the emails and messages I have received so far have helped me more than you know.

I hope Congress will treat my testimony responsibly and fairly, and do its due diligence to hear from other necessary witnesses. I hope the Office of Special Counsel and the inspectors general will step up to better protect me and my team. But if I can't count on either of those, at least I know the American people who listen to me will understand why I had to blow the whistle.

To the American people who this body works for, I implore you to look at the facts, not agenda-laced statements from either side of the aisle. I am the average American citizen who worries about how I will send my kids to college and if I will ever have enough money to retire, just like most people watching this.

I am the first person in my family to go to college. It was not an Ivy League school, and I don't have a network of rich and powerful friends to help me weather the storms of retaliation and character assassination raging on me for doing the right thing. I am putting myself at risk for the American people who support me and for those who do not. At the end of the day, I am just a small-town kid from Norwich, New York, who worked hard to get where I am and will never compromise my integrity. I will never forget who I am, where I come from, or all the people in my life who have made me who I am today.

With those statements out of the way, we began taking questions. Fielding questions from members of Congress, we did the best we could to stop things from going off the rails. We didn't always succeed, such as when Representative Marjorie Taylor Greene pulled up large pictures from Hunter's laptop of him doing drugs with naked women. Looking at them, Joe no longer had any doubt about which clips from the hearing would lead cable news that evening. He felt like thanking Congresswoman Greene for taking the heat off him, if only for a moment. Other questions came from Democrats seeking to discredit us. One of them, for reasons we didn't quite understand, displayed a large image of Rudy Giuliani with black hair dye streaming down his face. Another asked us repeatedly whether Joe Biden had been the president during the start of the investigation, believing that getting us to say "no" would prove some kind of point. It didn't, of course. Alexandria Ocasio-Cortez spent most of her time attacking President Trump on unrelated matters, doing what we'd been warned some members of Congress would do.

The few Democrats who tried to engage us on substance quickly found that they were outmatched. During one exchange, Representative Dan Goldman referred to the text message between

Hunter Biden and his Chinese business associate, claiming that it did not show that Hunter Biden was in business with his father. Gary shot back, "No, but it does show that Hunter Biden talked to his father about business." He knew that this contradicted statements from both the president and Hunter Biden, and it was no surprise to him that the congressman attempted to cut him off before he could finish the sentence.

This, in Gary's opinion, was emblematic of the problem with the way the hearing was conducted. The Democrats on the panel knew what the truth was. They could read the reams of documents we'd provided, just like the Republicans. Some of them, it seemed, even *had* read these documents. They knew there was no refuting the story we were here to tell. So they immediately switched into defense mode. They didn't care about the truth. They only cared about circling the wagons and protecting the blue team. The American people could see that.

During the first of many breaks, Joe checked his phone to find supportive messages from old friends and family members. There were at least four hundred of them. His brothers told him his head looked big. One of his brothers sent screenshots of strange websites that posted images of his children, listing them as "relatives of the IRS whistleblower." He flagged this to follow up on later. No one in leadership at the IRS said a thing. Before he knew it, the hearing was over, just a blur in his head that he'd have to watch later if he wanted to remember what happened.

Standing back outside the room, we shook hands with more members of Congress. We also met a few other staffers who'd helped coordinate our hearing and thanked them. Then Dean Zerbe took both of us and our legal team out to dinner at a steakhouse near the Capitol.

The press coverage of our testimony was pretty extensive, and the next morning, images of us sitting at the table speaking were printed in newspapers. And aside from a few left-leaning outlets, things looked pretty good. A report in *Axios*, which had included us in its "Driving the News" section, said, "House Republicans' investigations into the Biden family have thus far failed to convince a skeptical public, often plagued by unreliable witnesses and appearances of overt partisanship. But Wednesday's sworn testimony by Shapley and Ziegler—two career, nonpartisan officials with no obvious axe to grind—raised serious allegations that so far have gone unanswered by the Justice Department."

Most of the other straight news sites ran similar stories. Reading them, we were glad to see that we weren't being painted as partisan hacks looking to take down the Biden family by any means necessary. Most reasonable people understood what we were trying to do. Moving forward, we tried to limit the amount of media that we did. It was important that we didn't oversaturate things or appear to be reaching for our fifteen minutes of fame. If anything, we wanted the spotlight to move on from us as quickly as possible; the important thing was the story, and whatever we could do to highlight that, the better.

When it came to media outlets, we tried to take a balanced approach. Although we had inboxes full of requests from right-wing outlets, the first interview Joe gave after the House oversight hearing was to CNN. Speaking with Jake Tapper for about fifteen minutes, he ran through the facts of the case again, fielding questions and trying to lay things out as plainly as possible. Then, as it happened, he left on a preplanned trip for Europe, hoping things would calm down while he was away. Sitting on hotel balconies with fruity drinks in his hand, he checked in on his laptop on the media hits Gary was doing, watching with pride as his supervisor (who'd become one of his closest friends in the world) stayed strong and kept fighting.

The trip gave Joe a chance to read through some of the emails and text messages he'd gotten after the testimony. The most touching, of course, were from his friends. But he also liked the ones from Washington insiders, some of whom had seen dozens of whistleblowers come forward to report wrongdoing at their respective agencies. According to one of these insiders, the testimony that we gave that day in July was the most "believable" he'd ever seen. He pointed out that unlike most people, we managed not to get attacked for political posts.

There were also some posts that weren't as encouraging. Some people attacked us on Twitter, particularly Joe, who was more active on the platform. One of the strangest lines of attack came from the far left, which asserted (hilariously) that Joe must have been related to Garrett Ziegler, the right-wing psycho who'd accused him six months earlier of being a gay, Biden-loving Democrat trying to tank the Hunter Biden case to keep the case from ever moving forward. The first time around, when Garrett Ziegler had come at Joe from the right, the IRS had been all over the threats. So had the FBI. Leadership had checked in with him often, making sure he was kept updated on all the menacing emails that were coming in about him—photos of his home, death threats, and other shocking materials.

Now that he was a whistleblower, the IRS was dead silent.

The threats were piling up, and Joe had no one on his side to help deal with them—not that he'd had much use for the people on his side in the first place.

And, to make matters worse, it was time to go back to work.

ELEVEN

AFTERMATH

THE HARDEST PART about being a whistleblower is the public scrutiny. There's no denying that. Having millions of people around the country all suddenly thinking things about you one way or the other is not a comfortable feeling, especially if you've spent all your life up to that point as a private citizen.

The second worst part, without question, is going back to work.

For some reason, you don't think as much about this part. You want to get your ducks in a row so you can come forward, and then you want to make sure your testimony is perfect. You want to do all the interviews you think you need to do in order to get your message out, and you want to make sure people are discussing your case in the right way. All the while, you push away the thought that eventually you're going to have to sit back at your desk and pass all the people you just testified about in the hallways.

Gary had gone back to work almost immediately, trying to move forward as if nothing had happened. And after his trip, Joe returned to the office in August 2023, about three weeks after he'd testified. As much as we wanted to move on and begin working the next cases (hopefully ones that didn't involve the children of any corrupt politicians), the Sportsman case wasn't finished yet.

And there had been some major developments.

On July 26, about a week after our testimony, Hunter Biden had entered a federal courthouse in Delaware. After many months of back and forth between Christopher Clark and the U.S. Attorney's Office, which had often become extremely contentious, it seemed that the plea deal was finally going to go through. This deal, we knew, was extremely favorable to Hunter Biden. The pushback from the U.S. Attorney's Office had been embarrassingly weak. The judge, a Trump appointee named Maryellen Noreika, was expected to approve it quickly.

But things had changed since June, when the plea deal was put together. After our testimony, the case was now leading the nightly news. People from all over the political spectrum were now beginning to see that this case was not just about Hunter Biden, but also the principle of equal justice under the law. They had watched Democrats flail at the hearing to protect the Biden family, and the spectacle had disgusted them. Still, it was clear as Hunter strode into the courtroom that he still expected the case to go away. So did his lawyers, whose faces looked serene as they stood beside him facing the judge.

Things did not go their way.

From the moment the judge called the room to order, it was clear that she was not going to approve the agreement without asking a few questions. She was not, as she would put it near the end of the hearing, going to "rubber stamp" such a momentous agreement—especially not one that seemed to have been put together with so little care and forethought. The first signs of trouble came when Judge Noreika asked a few basic questions about the deal. First she dealt with the structure, noting that the agreement had been split into two parts—a plea and a diversion deal—instead of a unified document under the court's full authority. Then came the more unusual twist: the diversion agreement assigned her, the judge, the responsibility of determining whether its terms had been violated, even though neither the prosecution nor the defense could point to a single case where a judge had ever been given that role.

According to the way the agreement was written, that sweeping immunity wasn't laid out in the plea agreement—the document that would come under Judge Noreika's review. Instead, it was tucked away in the diversion agreement, a document that typically doesn't require judicial approval at all. In other words, the most consequential term in the entire deal—the government's commitment not to pursue additional charges against Hunter Biden—was deliberately placed in the one part of the agreement the judge wasn't supposed to touch.

This raised a host of red flags. In any standard plea negotiation, the scope of the deal—the charges the defendant is pleading guilty to, what charges are being dropped, and what conduct is being immunized—is spelled out plainly. That's how it works. That's how it's supposed to work. Not only does that give the judge a clear picture of what's being agreed to, it also ensures transparency for the public. But this deal seemed designed to obscure the real terms from judicial oversight—and from anyone else paying attention.

Judge Noreika quickly picked up on this. She asked the prosecutors directly whether there were any precedents for a judge playing the role she was being assigned under the diversion agreement—specifically, being the one to determine whether Hunter had violated the terms of that agreement in the future. Both sides admitted they couldn't name a single example of a judge ever being placed in that role. It was unprecedented. And once that door opened, things started unraveling fast.

The prosecution tried to argue that this unusual structure was necessary. Their justification? That a future Justice Department—presumably under Republican leadership—might try to allege a breach of the diversion agreement and bring new charges against Hunter Biden for political reasons. So, they said, the judge needed to be the firewall. But this logic didn't sit well with Noreika. She rightly pointed out that placing a federal judge in the position of approving—or blocking—future criminal charges could raise serious separation-of-powers concerns. That's not what federal judges are supposed to do. Deciding whether or not to bring charges is an executive branch function, not a judicial one.

Then came the most explosive moment: when Judge Noreika drilled down on the scope of the immunity Hunter was being promised. She asked if the investigation into Biden's potential violations of the Foreign Agents Registration Act (FARA) was still ongoing. The prosecutors said yes, it was. But Biden's attorneys took a very different view. They insisted that the immunity provisions already covered any potential FARA violations. In other words, they believed Hunter couldn't be charged for anything related to his extensive business dealings with foreign entities, including those in China, Romania, and Ukraine, because all of that was swept into the immunity clause.

To say this caught the judge's attention would be an understatement. Here was a defendant pleading guilty to two minor tax charges, with a recommended sentence of probation—and yet his lawyers were claiming that the deal protected him from prosecution for a wide range of other serious offenses. And somehow, those protections were hidden in a document that the court wasn't even supposed to have the power to review.

Noreika called for a break. When the parties returned to the courtroom, they tried to walk things back. The prosecution clarified that Hunter could, in fact, still be charged with FARA violations. The defense, now clearly on the back foot, nodded along. But it was too late. The damage was done. The judge had seen that not only were the parties not on the same page—they weren't even in the same book.

To us, it looked like a last-ditch effort to salvage the deal after being caught trying to sneak a blanket immunity clause past the court. But Judge Noreika wasn't biting. She continued to press the issue of her role in determining whether Hunter had violated the diversion agreement—something no judge had ever been asked to do. And she made clear that she believed the structure of the deal was so irregular, and potentially unconstitutional, that she could not approve it without additional briefing and clarification.

She asked the parties a simple question: would Hunter still be willing to enter into the plea agreement if she struck the provision assigning her the power to decide future breaches? Everyone in the courtroom understood what the answer was.

And that was that.

The plea deal was put on hold, and the parties were ordered to submit further legal arguments on the constitutional questions raised by the judge.

The sweetheart deal—which had been negotiated while neither of us was in the room—was effectively dead.

At the beginning of August, David Weiss formally requested special counsel authority (and not for the first time, as Gary knew). Attorney General Merrick Garland granted him this authority on August 11.

This time, Garland had no choice.

A few weeks before David Weiss came to Merrick Garland seeking special counsel authority, other news had broken regarding former presidents and legal problems. But they had nothing to do with the Biden family.

Special Counsel Jack Smith, who'd been looking into President Trump's handling of classified documents as well as his actions on January 6, 2021, among other things, had filed indictments against the former president. Unlike the teams we had worked on, these prosecutors had charged ahead with no delays, interviewing hundreds of witnesses and serving enough subpoenas to fill a storage unit in Northern Virginia. The classified documents case had included a raid on Mar-a-Lago, the former president's home, during which dozens of FBI agents had busted down doors and raided the place looking for materials related to the case.

No one had seriously raised the objection that investigating a former president during primary season might get anyone into "hot water." No one, to our knowledge, had wondered aloud whether "the juice wouldn't be worth the squeeze." The Department of Justice—the same Department of Justice that had wrung its hands about investigating the son of a potential candidate for president back in 2018—seemed just fine with investigating someone who had *been* president and could potentially be again.

Around this time, it became clearer than ever to us that the reticence of our superiors to bring a case against Hunter Biden had very little to do with protecting Hunter himself from prosecution.

Leadership at the Department of Justice couldn't have cared less whether Hunter ended up in prison for his crimes. What they cared about was making sure that Joe Biden wasn't politically weakened to the extent that Donald Trump could eventually become president again.

Having served around government bureaucrats for many years—who, in the end, are the ones who can make or break cases—we know what makes them tick. We know what they like, and we know what they're afraid of. And around 2023, what they were afraid of more than anything else was the prospect of a second Trump presidency. This fear only grew as Trump began rising in the polls, making promises that if he won the White House again, he would slash federal agencies, gut the administrative state, and demand that government workers come back to the office full time, among other things.

Government workers would rather break every ethical norm in the book—some even going so far as to break the law—to prevent that from happening. The ethos seemed to be: *anyone but Trump.* If that meant Biden, the bureaucracy—which, in effect, functions more like a living, breathing organism than a group of individuals—would protect Biden. If it meant Nancy Pelosi, the bureaucracy would rally around her instead. The only thing that was unacceptable to these people was having the man who'd vowed to dismantle the bureaucracy come to power again.

And in the summer of 2023, it seemed they were well on their way to accomplishing that goal. The classified documents indictment appeared ironclad, carefully constructed, and aggressively pursued. The January 6 indictment was so sprawling, so full of legal complexity and historical weight, that it looked like it would tie up Trump's legal team—and the candidate himself—for years to come.

The Department of Justice no longer had the ability to claim that it wanted to stay out of politics. It had, in fact, inserted itself right into the political process right at the moment when the 2024 presidential race was beginning to heat up, and it had done so in a way that all but ensured President Trump's court cases would coincide with his campaign for president. Even to American citizens who knew nothing about politics, it was clear that the DOJ had acted to hamper the former president's chances of winning the White House again.

All the while, more testimony came out of the House of Representatives, which—between the Ways and Means Committee, the Oversight Committee, and the Judiciary Committee—seemed determined to interview everyone who'd worked on the Sportsman case. One of the first interview subjects was a special agent at the FBI whose name was redacted in the documents Chairman Comer released. But the substance of the testimony backed up everything we'd said in front of the committee—down to the last detail.

Among these details were confirmations that the FBI had, in fact, notified Secret Service headquarters and the Biden transition team the night before we were scheduled to interview Hunter Biden—just as we'd testified. "I know I was upset when I learned about it," the agent told Oversight Committee staff. "I felt it was people that did not need to know about our intent."

He confirmed the original plan was to notify the local Secret Service field office on the morning of the interview—not the night before, and certainly not via FBI headquarters in D.C. When asked why that plan had changed, he admitted that he had been informed that FBI headquarters had gone ahead and made the call. "I didn't understand why the initial notification," he said plainly.

He also confirmed how that tip-off changed everything. "I was notified by my assistant special agent in charge that we would not even be allowed to approach the house," he testified. Instead, the plan became to hand over his contact information to the Secret Service and wait for Hunter to call him. "In your twenty-year career," one committee staffer asked him, "have you ever been told that you had to wait outside of a target's home until they contacted you?" His response: "Not that I recall."

In the months to come, similar testimony would come out. And not a single line of it would damage what we'd said in front of the committee that day in July. The picture of just how badly the Department of Justice had conducted itself during the Sportsman investigation was becoming clearer every day. So was the picture of the Biden family's obvious attempts to peddle its influence overseas. With every interview and document that came out, the Hunter Biden camp became more distressed. That September, on the strength of all this information, the House announced that it had begun an official impeachment inquiry against President Biden.

It was clear by now that the Biden legal team could not beat us on the facts. After five years of working this case nonstop, Joe knew it about as well as he knew anything. Even Gary, who'd been supervising dozens of other cases at the time Sportsman was being investigated, now knew every line item in the case files almost by heart. Everyone involved in the case—from the judges to the prosecutors, the special agents, and the lawyers for Hunter Biden—seemed to understand that the evidence against him was irrefutable. It didn't matter how many bulldog lawyers he threw at the matter.

So the team resorted to one last-ditch effort to get us to shut up.

They sued.

It wasn't like we hadn't seen this coming.

All throughout the fall of 2022, when Gary was deciding whether to come forward, his greatest fear had been that he might someday be prosecuted for illegally disclosing taxpayer information. Joe had gone through the same thought process. In the end, we'd been assured that as long as we went about things in the correct manner, we'd be complying with the law and would be safe from prosecution.

Still, it didn't feel great when we learned on September 18, 2023, that Hunter Biden was suing the IRS, alleging that we had improperly released his tax information in an attempt "to embarrass and inflict harm" on him. In addition to claiming that our first release of information was illegal—which we knew was nonsense, given the protections we had under whistleblower statutes—Biden's lawyers claimed that the comments we'd made in the media and during our congressional testimony had gone "well outside the bounds of the whistleblower protections we enjoyed."

Again, this was BS. But we'd dealt with the Hunter Biden legal team enough to know that they were going to come at us guns blazing whether their charges were BS or not. We needed good legal representation—someone who was willing to fight it out with us in court. And because it was the IRS that was being sued, it was up to the lawyers at the IRS to mount a good defense. Over the course of the next few months, they consistently failed to do this. For one thing, they did not move to dismiss the charges against us, as any good defense lawyers would have done. And they refused to allow us to have any input into our own defense strategy. It made sense, of course. We were being defended by the very people we'd just blown the whistle on.

All the while, we were still under attack. One of Hunter Biden's attorneys, Abbe Lowell, seemed particularly focused on discrediting us publicly. From early on, it was clear that his approach wasn't limited to defending his client in court—he wanted to go after us directly. Throughout the year, as the case progressed, Lowell issued statements and letters accusing us of wrongdoing, often mischaracterizing our actions and motives in the process.

At one point, he claimed we had committed a "clear-cut crime" by disclosing confidential taxpayer information—an accusation that ignored the fact that our disclosures were made lawfully under the protections afforded to whistleblowers by Congress. In public and private communications, he alleged that we had violated grand jury secrecy rules and broken federal law. He described us as disgruntled agents airing grievances rather than professionals raising legitimate concerns. And he didn't keep those comments confined to the courtroom. He made the accusations in letters to federal agencies, including the Biden administration, and encouraged them to take action against us. When we later tried to intervene in the IRS lawsuit in order to respond, both the IRS and Lowell opposed our motion—effectively arguing that Lowell should be allowed to make accusations in court without giving us the chance to defend ourselves.

Lowell's tactics went beyond legal defense. His public stature and aggressive messaging made it harder to cut through the noise and get people to focus on the facts. To many in the media and the public, it created the impression of a dispute between two sides slinging accusations at each other—when in reality, we were simply pointing out what had happened during an investigation that was supposed to be free from political influence. The longer it went on, the clearer it became that we weren't just up against legal arguments—we were up against a strategy designed to make an example out of us.

And we weren't the only ones. Over the next few months, as his prospects for wriggling out of what he'd done dwindled down to nothing, Hunter would have his legal team sue just about everyone who'd ever said anything negative about him in public. He came at Rudy Giuliani, Garrett Ziegler, and Mac Isaac, knowing that as long as he threw enough money and tough lawyers at the situation, he'd probably be able to win at least something in court. It was yet another example of the Biden family way. Hunter knew that money gave him power, and he used that power to attack people who didn't have half the resources that he did. It was ironic that one of those people was Garrett Ziegler, the former Trump White House aide who'd outed Joe as a gay Democrat on the assumption that Joe would try to tank the Hunter Biden case. A few months before that, Garrett Ziegler—again, no relation—had been among the first people to leak contents of the Hunter Biden laptop online.

Like Democrats in Congress, Hunter seemed to have accepted that he could no longer win on the facts. With his plea deal in tatters and the eyes of just about every American in the country on his case, it was becoming clear to him that for once, he wasn't going to be able to escape the consequences of his actions. So he lashed out on everything he could think of *other* than the facts, blaming the people who had correctly noticed he'd broken the law and trying to ruin them by throwing what seemed to be endless amounts of money at the cases. By now, a great deal of Hunter's income came from selling paintings, often to people who appeared to want to purchase influence with the Biden family. It was the clearest indication yet that even after so many years of being investigated for corrupt business dealings, he had no intention of changing his ways.

And his actions were finally catching up to him.

This became clearer than ever on December 7, 2023, when David Weiss's office announced that a grand jury had charged Hunter Biden with three felony tax offenses and six misdemeanors.

Reading the indictment, Joe was proud to see that it was entirely based on the work he'd done for five years. On every page there was something that sparked a memory: a calculation he'd done at his kitchen table while the rest of his family was celebrating Thanksgiving, a line from an interview he'd flown halfway across the country to conduct, and dozens of small leads he'd followed up on over the course of his investigation, often against the advice of his superiors and the DOJ. Without his work and his determination to push forward, this indictment wouldn't have existed. That day in December, he found himself reading the first few pages over and over again, having trouble believing that justice was finally on the verge of being served.

As David Weiss's office had put it:

> At times relevant to this Indictment:
> Defendant ROBERT HUNTER BIDEN (hereafter "the Defendant") was a Georgetown- and Yale-educated lawyer, lobbyist, consultant, and businessperson and, beginning in April 2018, a resident of Los Angeles, California.

At times relevant to this Indictment, the Defendant served on the board of a Ukrainian industrial conglomerate and a Chinese private equity fund. He negotiated and executed contracts and agreements for business and legal services that paid millions of dollars of compensation to him and/or his domestic corporations, Owasco, PC and Owasco, LLC.

In addition to his business interests, the Defendant was an employee of a multi-national law firm working in an "of counsel" capacity from 2009 through at least 2017.

The Defendant engaged in a four-year scheme to not pay at least $1.4 million in self-assessed federal taxes he owed for tax years 2016 through 2019, from in or about January 2017 through in or about October 15, 2020, and to evade the assessment of taxes for tax year 2018 when he filed false returns in or about February 2020. In furtherance of that scheme, the Defendant: subverted the payroll and tax withholding process of his own company, Owasco, PC by withdrawing millions from Owasco, PC outside of the payroll and tax withholding process that it was designed to perform; spent millions of dollars on an extravagant lifestyle rather than paying his tax bills; in 2018, stopped paying his outstanding and overdue taxes for tax year 2015; willfully failed to pay his 2016, 2017, 2018, and 2019 taxes on time, despite having access to funds to pay some or all of these taxes; willfully failed to file his 2017 and 2018 tax returns on time; and when he did finally file his 2018 returns, included false business deductions in order to evade assessment of taxes to reduce the substantial tax liabilities he faced as of February 2020.

There it was, all laid out in a legal document in clear language that anyone could understand. There were times when it seemed a little silly to be so happy that this had finally happened, at least to Joe. Having some spoiled rich kid finally brought to justice wasn't exactly solving world hunger.

But to a veteran criminal investigator, the moment this indictment came down stood for something much bigger. In a sense, it was even more momentous than the moment Hunter finally pled guilty to these charges nearly a full year later (after once again attempting to plead not guilty, of course). The indictment signaled to the people of the United States that it didn't matter what a person's last name was or how many high-powered lawyers they could afford to employ. People who committed crimes in the United States were going to be held to account. During the worst parts of the Sportsman investigation, whenever we felt like quitting, we would keep in mind just how many people in the United States pay their taxes and follow the law, even when they don't want to.

Throughout the case, Hunter Biden attempted to blame substance abuse and family crises for the illegal things he had done. But there's hardly a person in the world who doesn't go through struggles. Over the course of this case, we'd seen our fair share. Gary had agonized for months over his decision to come forward. He began confiding in close friends and coordinating with his local police department to deal with the hate and death threats that often came at him as a result of his decision to come forward. Joe had lost his mother-in-law while working the case. He'd endured months of strain on his marriage while trying to move things across the finish line, and he'd dealt with serious threats from both sides of the political aisle when he decided to come forward as a whistleblower. In November 2023, he learned that his father's cancer had spread to his brain, leaving him with only a few months to live.

And through all of that, we'd both managed to pay our taxes.

So had millions of Americans all over the country, some of whom deal with the kind of struggles that Hunter Biden could hardly imagine. We didn't fall back on excuses to explain why we spent the money we should have paid in taxes on crack, hookers, and a Porsche. We submitted our tax returns by April 15 every year because we knew that if we didn't, we'd get in serious trouble.

Exactly the kind of trouble that Hunter Biden finally, after nearly a decade of trying to wriggle out of it, found himself in as we headed toward the end of 2023.

Meanwhile, at the office, we suffered greatly for our decision to come forward. Even though the retaliation wasn't official, we could tell that our careers at the IRS—the agency to which we'd both devoted a great deal of our adult lives—were going to suffer as a result of what we'd done. Gary was denied promotions, and we were kept out of the loop on cases and sidelined in a hundred small ways. As all this was happening, Gary looked into the rules of the IRS and found that at the agency, past performance was no guarantee of future success; promotions were decided based on how long someone had been there, not how many successful cases they had worked.

This was wrong. But there wasn't much we could do about it.

For a while, we tried to put things back together in our personal lives. Gary got back into the swing of things, apologizing to his wife and daughters for how much stress he'd caused them over the past few years. Joe spent time with his father, who was declining quickly, and tried to come to some resolution about all they'd been through together. Near the end, Joe's father told him how proud he'd been watching him testify that July; he said he was proud to see him out there being who he was, unafraid of what was going to happen to him. When he died in January 2024, Joe felt that they'd finally worked things out, if such a thing is really possible. He even gave the eulogy at his father's memorial service.

There were other moments of closure. During a vacation to Portugal in May 2024, the same place David had been while Joe was testifying, Joe and David decided to call it quits on their marriage. Joe quickly moved to end his marriage, sad that it was over but optimistic about moving on. In July 2024, he began seeing someone new, looking forward to picking up the pieces from his life with someone who was a breath of fresh air to him—someone who continually stood by his side when things got rough and helped show Joe, again, what true love looked like.

All the while, a presidential race between Joe Biden and Donald Trump raged. It was clear to everyone watching that Biden, who had never exactly been at a 100 percent during his time in office, wasn't going to make it. Aside from the fact that he was obviously in a state of mental decline, the scandals surrounding his family were piling up. The impeachment inquiry seemed to have turned up irrefutable evidence (some of it provided by us) that Biden was a full participant in the schemes his brother and son had been coming up with for decades. And while they'd done the best they could to hide the involvement of "the Big Guy," they wouldn't be able to do it for long.

We weren't surprised that President Trump did so well against Joe Biden in the beginning of the race. In a way, Trump represented a clear repudiation of everything Biden had stood for these past four years: corruption, secrecy, and inequal justice under the law. The Department of Justice had come at Trump with everything it had, fast-tracking the cases against him rather than trying to make them go away. And Trump had beaten back everything, even as he showed up to court and endured some of the worst publicity in the history of American politics. The American people stood behind him because they had seen just how tilted our justice system had become. They knew that under Joe Biden, things were set up to protect Democrats and make sure Republicans (Trump especially) never returned to power.

The only way to fight that kind of corrupt system, it seemed, was with strength. This is exactly what we had in mind in September 2024 when we brought a $20 million lawsuit against Abbe Lowell for defamation. In the case, we alleged that this well-known, well-connected attorney had launched a sustained campaign of falsehoods designed to destroy our reputations and intimidate anyone else who might think about blowing the whistle.

We weren't exaggerating. The complaint, filed in the U.S. District Court for the District of Columbia, laid out exactly how Lowell had tried to make examples of us—not by contesting the facts of the case, but by smearing our names in the press and accusing us of committing crimes we did not commit. We were both current federal agents, still working on behalf of the taxpayers, when Lowell falsely stated—repeatedly and publicly—that we had committed felonies.

Lowell accused us of "illegal disclosure of grand jury materials and taxpayer return information," even though he knew that we had "never publicly discussed return information that was not already public." He called our actions "clear-cut crimes" that were "not protected by any whistleblower statute or other federal law." Our complaint explained how Lowell told Congress and the media that our disclosures were felonies—even though they had been made legally and with full authorization from the appropriate congressional committees.

It was one thing for a lawyer to defend his client. It was another for him to accuse two federal agents of criminal conduct. It was another still to amplify those accusations in a way that would cause as much reputational damage as possible. As we explained in the complaint, "Lowell's stature and credibility in the legal community have amplified the harm caused by his defamatory statements." Our lawsuit explained that these weren't careless remarks. They were deliberate—and malicious.

Lowell's most egregious step came on September 14, 2023, when he sent a letter to several congressional committees and simultaneously released it to the public. In doing so, he republished a number of prior communications—including letters from fellow Biden attorney Christopher Clark—that were filled with allegations we believe he knew were false. According to the filing, these included accusations that we "leaked information to the press, apparently in violation of federal law," that we had "committed felonies," and that our conduct had caused "irreversible damage." One of the republished letters even accused Gary of being "the source of at least many of the most damaging and troubling leaks," while another called Joe "yet another federal agent [who] illegally leaked information protected by Rule 6(e) and Section 6103." These allegations were completely untrue.

Lowell even wrote to U.S. attorney David Weiss, falsely asserting that we had "illegally disclosed grand jury and tax return information," and that our disclosures were "quite simply crimes." His letter described us as having committed "knowing violations of the law that constitute contempt and felony crimes."

Every single one of these statements was defamatory. They weren't vague criticisms or differences of opinion. They were direct, categorical accusations of criminal behavior—made with full knowledge that what we had done was lawful. As the complaint states, Lowell knew that whistleblower disclosures of confidential tax information to congressional tax committees are fully authorized by law. He knew we hadn't violated any grand jury rules. He made the claims anyway.

And so, on September 13, 2024—one day short of a year from Lowell's letter—we filed suit. We asked the court for damages—not just to compensate for the reputational harm, the shame, and the mental anguish, but to make a point. As the filing put it, "Lowell's conduct as alleged herein was willful, wanton, and malicious and was done with conscious disregard for [our] rights. Accordingly, an award of punitive and exemplary damages is appropriate."

The message was simple. You don't get to lie about whistleblowers just because the truth they told made your client uncomfortable. You don't get to turn federal law on its head because the facts are not in your favor. And you certainly don't get to smear the reputations of two men who followed the law, respected the rules, and did their jobs with integrity.

Not without a fight.

As of this writing, that lawsuit is still ongoing. But Hunter Biden's are not.

Hunter Biden continued to pursue his lawsuit against the IRS long after dropping nearly every other legal action, claiming he lacked the funds to continue them. But in April 2025, he dropped that one, too—voluntarily dismissing the case with prejudice, just as our legal team was preparing to intervene and present our defense. His lawsuit had always been an attempt to intimidate us for telling the truth, and in the end, it collapsed under its own weight. We never got our day in court, but the dismissal told the public everything they needed to know.

Of course, other things have changed, too.

TWELVE

BIG CHANGES

ON DECEMBER 1, just over five months after he dropped out of the presidential race and three weeks after his chosen successor lost to Donald Trump in a landslide, Joe Biden made an announcement. In true Biden fashion, the announcement wasn't about the health of the country or any of the initiatives he'd tried to pass while in office. It was about a member of the Biden crime family.

Specifically, Hunter, who had by now pled guilty to all charges David Weiss had brought against him.

"Today, I have signed a full pardon for my son Hunter," President Biden said in a statement, which continued:

> From the day I took office, I said I would not interfere with the Justice Department's decision-making, and I kept my word even as I have watched my son being selectively, and unfairly, prosecuted. Without aggravating factors like use in a crime, multiple purchases, or buying a weapon as a straw purchaser, people are almost never brought to trial on felony charges solely for how they filled out a gun form. Those who were late paying their

taxes because of serious addictions, but paid them back subsequently with interest and penalties, are typically given non-criminal resolutions. It is clear that Hunter was treated differently.

The charges in his cases came about only after several of my political opponents in Congress instigated them to attack me and oppose my election. Then, a carefully negotiated plea deal, agreed to by the Department of Justice, unraveled in the court room—with a number of my political opponents in Congress taking credit for bringing political pressure on the process. Had the plea deal held, it would have been a fair, reasonable resolution of Hunter's cases.

No reasonable person who looks at the facts of Hunter's cases can reach any other conclusion than Hunter was singled out only because he is my son—and that is wrong. There has been an effort to break Hunter—who has been five and a half years sober, even in the face of unrelenting attacks and selective prosecution. In trying to break Hunter, they've tried to break me—and there's no reason to believe it will stop here. Enough is enough.

For my entire career I have followed a simple principle: just tell the American people the truth. They'll be fair-minded. Here's the truth: I believe in the justice system, but as I have wrestled with this, I also believe raw politics has infected this process and it led to a miscarriage of justice—and once I made this decision this weekend, there was no sense in delaying it further. I hope Americans will understand why a father and a president would come to this decision.

Many Americans, especially those working in the media, were shocked by this statement. We were not. After more than five years of digging through the correspondence of the Biden family, witnessing the self-dealing and willingness to bend the law firsthand, we could see this pardon coming a mile away.

Still, it's worth pointing out all the outright lies in Joe Biden's statement. First and foremost, the plea deal Hunter was offered would not have represented a "fair, reasonable resolution" to the case. No other taxpayer would have gotten such a favorable deal. In fact, as we pointed out dozens of times throughout this book, any other taxpayer would have been interviewed within thirty days of Joe realizing that he or she hadn't paid or filed their taxes, then potentially charged shortly after that.

Hunter was not singled out because he was Joe Biden's son. In fact, the case was brought *despite* the fact that Hunter was Joe Biden's son—a fact that would have made the case go away if it hadn't been for our efforts to keep it alive. The only special treatment Hunter received throughout the process, in fact, came on December 1, when his father used the power of the presidency to nullify Hunter's guilty plea for tax crimes and jury conviction for gun crimes.

In the following days, many people pointed out just how many times Joe Biden had sworn he'd never do such a thing. We've already mentioned one earlier in this book when Biden swore all the way back in 2019 that he wouldn't dream of issuing pardons to members of his family.

He also said it repeatedly while in office.

In June 2023, when ABC's David Muir asked him directly if he would rule out pardoning his son, Biden replied, simply, "Yes." A few days later, at a news conference, he doubled down: "I said I'd abide by the jury decision. I will do that. And I will not pardon him." He added that he wouldn't commute the sentence either. Around the same time, he released a statement insisting, "I am the president, but I am also a dad. I love our son, and we are so proud of the man he is today . . . I will accept the outcome of this case and will continue to respect the judicial process." Even his press secretary, Karine Jean-Pierre, made it clear. In July, when asked whether the president would ever consider a pardon for his son, she answered, "No." And when asked again in November, she said, "Our answer stands, which is no."

Throughout history, presidents have used the pardon power very sparingly. The decisions are bound to invite controversy. This is why most pardons are signed in the final hours of the presidency as Marine One is waiting on the lawn to whisk the president away back to private life. In this way, at least, the Hunter Biden pardon was surprising. It was issued when there was still more than a month left in President Biden's first and only term. Looking back, we might assume that Biden wanted to issue the pardon before David Weiss could issue his full report on the matter, which has become customary for special counsels.

Weiss's report failed to answer virtually all of the questions Congress had posed to him about his own office's handing of the Hunter Biden investigation. But Weiss did take the time to highlight in the report falsehoods in the attacks on his office from the Hunter Biden legal team.

And in a final section of the report, Weiss called President Biden's decision to pardon Hunter "gratuitous and wrong." He continued:

> Other presidents have pardoned family members, but in doing so, none have taken the occasion as an opportunity

to malign the public servants at the Department of Justice based solely on false accusations.

These prosecutions were the culmination of thorough, impartial investigations, not partisan politics. Eight judges across numerous courts have rejected claims that they were the result of selective or vindictive motives. Calling those rulings into question and injecting partisanship into the independent administration of the law undermines the very foundation of what makes America's justice system fair and equitable. It erodes public confidence in an institution that is essential to preserving the rule of law.

In prosecuting these cases, I exercised my best judgment in deciding whether we could prove the cases and whether there was a substantial federal interest. I recognize that reasonable minds may differ about the correctness of my decisions. What should not be questioned, however, is that these decisions were duly considered and made in good faith with fidelity to the Principles of Federal Prosecution. Far from selective, these prosecutions were the embodiment of the equal application of justice—no matter who you are, or what your last name is, you are subject to the same laws as everyone else in the United States.

But it soon became clear that the Hunter pardon was only a warm-up.

On January 20, at the very moment that President Trump was headed to the Capitol rotunda to deliver his second Inaugural Address, President Biden ordered a fresh group of pardons. Only these were preemptive, meaning they were issued before any charges had even been filed—effectively giving the recipients a legal shield in case they were ever investigated or prosecuted in the future.

The people who received these pardons included the usual suspects: Dr. Anthony Fauci, General Mark Milley, several staffers from the January 6th Committee, and a handful of U.S. Capitol Police officers who had testified against Trump. But President Biden also extended preemptive pardons to members of his own family—his brothers James and Francis, his sister Valerie, and their spouses.

In the statement announcing the pardons, President Biden insisted that the recipients had done nothing wrong, but that "extraordinary times call for extraordinary protections." He claimed that "political retribution has no place in our system of justice" and that the pardons were necessary to "protect public servants and private citizens alike from the threat of vindictive prosecution."

To us, this was the ultimate proof that the allegations others had been making for years—that the Bidens were undeniably a crime family peddling their influence overseas and getting giant sums of money to exercise their power in dubious ways—were true. If they weren't true, there would have been no need for Joe Biden to issue the pardons in the first place. And if Joe Biden wasn't ashamed of the fact that he was issuing these pardons, he wouldn't have done it on January 20, mere minutes before he was set to leave the White House, while nearly every news camera in the world was pointed at the Capitol rotunda.

However, there were some positive developments that day. Watching President Trump deliver his stirring second Inaugural Address, it was clear that our fight was not going to end with the inauguration of a new president. If anything, it was going to become more important than ever. Speaking to the people gathered in the Capitol rotunda that afternoon, President Trump addressed the weaponization of government that had occurred under his predecessor's watch—weaponization of which he had been the primary target. And he did it right at the top of his speech, signaling just how important it would be moving forward.

Under his administration, he said, "Our sovereignty will be reclaimed. Our safety will be restored. The scales of justice will be rebalanced. The vicious, violent, and unfair weaponization of the Justice Department and our government will end." A few minutes later, he said, "Never again will the immense power of the state be weaponized to persecute political opponents—something I know something about." The crowd laughed at this line, though the Democrats behind him did not. He continued, "We will not allow that to happen. It will not happen again. Under my leadership, we will restore fair, equal, and impartial justice under the constitutional rule of law."

It was one thing to say that, of course. It was quite another to make it happen. After all, every president before Trump had claimed that they were operating on the principle of equal justice under the law. Joe Biden had made this a major selling point for his candidacy back in 2019 when he was first running to replace President Trump. But as soon as it came time to put those principles into action, he proved that he cared much more about himself than he did about the principles he was professing.

President Trump had been different, especially when it came to government whistleblowers. In 2018, he had signed the Whistleblower Protection Coordination Act, which permanently reinstated the Whistleblower Ombudsman Program that had expired the previous year. The law required every federal agency's Office of Inspector General to maintain a whistleblower protection coordinator—someone responsible for educating federal employees about their rights to report wrongdoing and ensuring their complaints were handled quickly and thoroughly. It also reinforced coordination between agencies and Congress to make sure whistleblower disclosures were addressed appropriately.

Lawmakers have stood up for the protection of whistleblowers as well, and no one has been more strident about the issue than Senator Chuck Grassley. At every step of the way, Senator Grassley and his staff have assured us that we were doing the right thing by coming forward, and not only because we were working with some of his former congressional aides. He believes in the principles of transparency, accountability, and equal justice under the law—and he has fought for them even when doing so was not popular.

On February 14, 2025, Senator Grassley wrote to President Trump requesting that the White House hold a Rose Garden ceremony on Whistleblower Appreciation Day to honor those who risk their careers, reputations, and even their health to expose government wrongdoing. It was the kind of bold public statement Grassley had been pushing for since the Reagan administration—a visible and unmistakable sign that whistleblowers would be supported, not silenced.

"Whistleblowers have exposed waste, fraud and abuse in just about every industry and agency in this country," Grassley wrote. "The issues they report have saved billions of taxpayer dollars and countless more through their deterrent effect." He pointed to whistleblowers from the IRS, the DOJ, and the FBI—including those who had come forward to disclose misconduct in the Hunter Biden investigation—who had faced retaliation and efforts to destroy their careers. Honoring them at the highest level of government, he argued, would "inspire confidence in those who witness wrongdoing to stand up and do something to fix it."

Senator Grassley didn't just ask President Trump to praise whistleblowers in theory—he asked him to break the precedent of every president who came before and actually celebrate them in public. "Let whistleblowers smell the roses at the White House," Grassley wrote, "and bask in the appreciation of a thankful nation well served by their efforts to shine a light on waste, fraud, and abuse."

For most lawmakers, that would have been enough.

But Senator Grassley, who had gone above and beyond since the beginning, worked behind the scenes to ensure that the retaliation against us would end and that we would get back to doing work that matters.

On March 18, 2025, the Department of the Treasury announced that we had been promoted.

Gary was appointed deputy chief of the IRS Criminal Investigation Division and named a senior advisor to the treasury secretary, focusing on reform. Joe received a similar appointment, joining him in the secretary's office. We began the work immediately.

The news caught some people off guard. After all, we were the whistleblowers—ostracized, sidelined, and targeted for doing what we believed was right. For months, we had been warned that the decision to come forward might be the end of our careers. But instead of being pushed out, we were invited back in—not just as agents, but as leaders. Not just to do a job, but to help change a culture.

There are a lot of people to thank. The senator who's been a lifelong champion for whistleblowers. The secretary who decided to bring us on knowing exactly what kind of heat it might bring. And the president who made it clear from the beginning that standing up to wrongdoing would be rewarded, not punished.

We don't think of these new roles as rewards. We think of them as responsibilities.

The truth is, we still have a lot of work to do. The system isn't fixed. The people who tried to silence us haven't all been held accountable. And there are others—good, honest people working across the government—who are watching closely to see what happens next. If our story gives even one of them the courage to speak up, then it's worth it.

This chapter of our lives may be closing. But the mission continues.

And it's far from over.

ABOUT THE AUTHORS

GARY SHAPLEY grew up in Norwich, New York, and began his college career at Binghamton University before volunteering with AmeriCorps in Colorado. He later earned a BS in accounting and business administration from the University of Maryland and an MBA from the University of Baltimore. After interning at the Department of Defense, Gary worked in the Inspector General's Office at the NSA before joining IRS-Criminal Investigation (IRS-CI) in 2009. From 2013 to 2018, he was detailed to the DOJ Tax Division investigating foreign financial institutions, including Credit Suisse and HSBC PBRS as part of the Swiss Bank Program. He also worked on the Joint Terrorism Task Force (JTTF) at the FBI Washington and Baltimore Field Offices. In 2018, he was promoted to supervisory special agent in Baltimore and helped establish the Joint Chiefs of Global Tax Enforcement (J5), an international effort to combat financial crimes. He later led the International Tax and Financial Crimes (ITFC) group, overseeing elite agents specializing in complex tax fraud cases, and was recently promoted to Deputy Chief of IRS CI. He has also been detailed as a senior advisor working on IRS reform with the Secretary of the Treasury.

JOSEPH ZIEGLER grew up in Kirtland, Ohio, and graduated from Ohio University in 2007 with a BS in accounting. He worked as an external auditor at Ernst & Young LLP, handling clients like the Cleveland Clinic and Lincoln Electric, while earning his MBA from John Carroll University in 2009. Joe joined IRS-CI in 2010, specializing in healthcare fraud and prescription drug diversion. In 2016, he transferred to the Atlanta Field Office working on complex captive insurance tax shelter cases while serving as the public information officer. In November 2018, he initiated the Hunter Biden case and joined the International Tax and Financial Crimes group (ITFC) in Washington, D.C. Often called the "SEAL Team 6 of the IRS," this elite unit investigates high-level tax fraud and financial crimes worldwide. Joe was recently elevated as a senior advisor (detailee) by the Secretary of the Treasury.